Autobiography of Red Cloud

Red Cloud, ca. 1870s

Autobiography of Red Cloud

WAR LEADER OF THE OGLALAS

EDITED BY R. Eli Paul

MONTANA
HISTORICAL
SOCIETY
PRESS

COVER IMAGE Red Cloud, photograph by David F. Barry, 1897, courtesy Denver Public Library, Western History Department

FRONTISPIECE Red Cloud, ca. 1870s, courtesy Nebraska State Historical Society

COVER DESIGN BY Kathryn Fehlig

TYPESET IN ITC Galliard by Arrow Graphics, Missoula, Montana

PRINTED BY BookCrafters in Chelsea, Michigan

An earlier version of the introduction appeared as "Recovering Red Cloud's Autobiography," *Montana The Magazine of Western History* 44 (Summer 1994), 2–17.

98 99 00 01 02 03 04 05   9 8 7 6 5 4 3 2 1

Library of Congress Cataloging-in-Publication Data

Allen, Charles Wesley, 1851–1942.
   Autobiography of Red Cloud : war leader of the Oglalas / edited by R. Eli Paul.
      p. cm.
   Written by Charles Wesley Allen from Red Cloud's reminiscences told to Sam Deon, and repeated to Allen.
   Includes bibliographical references and index.
   ISBN 0-917298-49-7 (cloth : alk. paper) — ISBN 0-917298-50-0 (paper : alk. paper)
      1. Red Cloud, 1822–1909. 2. Oglala Indians—Kings and rulers—Biography. 3. Oglala Indians—Wars. 4. Oglala Indians—Government relations. I. Red Cloud, 1822–1909.
II. Deon, Sam. III. Paul, R. Eli, 1954– . IV. Title.
E99.03R372 1997
973'.04975'0092—dc21
[B]   96-52849
                                                              CIP

This book was made possible in part by funding
provided by the Montana Historical Society Foundation.

Contents

A teenage Red Cloud goes on his first raid, which is successful, against the Pawnees of Nebraska.

Warned of an approaching Crow raid, Red Cloud joins the men of his village to surprise and kill them. He counts three coups.

Camps of the Sioux and Omaha tribes encounter one another on disputed hunting grounds. Red Cloud and four companions charge the Omahas, and Red Cloud helps a wounded comrade from the field of battle.

Red Cloud shows great initiative and bravery as a member of a successful horse raid.

5. SHOSHONES 55

Leading a party of twelve men, Red Cloud captures sixty Shoshone horses. He counts coup on one adversary and kills and scalps him.

6. SHOOTING BULL BEAR 64

A deadly tribal feud climaxes in the killing of the Oglala chief Bull Bear by Red Cloud.

7. RAID ON THE PAWNEES 71

During an attack on a Pawnee village Red Cloud is wounded. His comrades help him return home safely.

8. MARRIAGE 76

In love with two women, Red Cloud chooses one to marry.

9. FAILURE 85

Black Eagle, an Oglala rival, leads a raid against the Crows. The foray meets with disaster.

10. SCALPED ALIVE 97

Red Cloud leads an avenging party to Crow country, where he finds a village and captures a nearby herd of horses. Red Cloud scalps an apparent Crow sentry.

11. THE PIPE DANCE 106

Red Cloud participates in a series of ceremonies that mark his entry into the upper echelons of Sioux society.

12. TO WHIP A DOG 112

Red Cloud beats a Cheyenne man accused of abusing a Sioux woman.

Preface

ON A LIBRARY SHELF at the Nebraska State Historical Society rests a bound manuscript titled "Life of Red Cloud." The author of the manuscript is Addison E. Sheldon, a former director of the Society. The 1932 manuscript, which consists of 134 typed, double-spaced pages, purports to be the life story of the Lakota chief Red Cloud, one of the West's most famous Native American figures. Historians have generally remained unaware of the Sheldon manuscript or have given it little credence, perhaps for good reason—until now.

"Life of Red Cloud," it turns out, was not written in 1932 but rather in 1893. Furthermore, the author was not Sheldon, who had only a passing acquaintance with the famed chief, but was instead Charles W. Allen, who had resided with Red Cloud on the Pine Ridge Reservation of South Dakota. The 1932 date appears because that was the year the manuscript was typed by Mari Sandoz, at the time Sheldon's assistant at the Nebraska State Historical Society and later a noted western writer. The document has a complex genealogy, which, using previously overlooked or restricted material in the Nebraska State Historical Society collections, can be traced with some certainty.

The document's saga began in 1893 at the Pine Ridge post office, where Red Cloud and Sam Deon, his long-time friend, would sit and reminisce. Deon easily coaxed from the old man stories of his early years. Then, without Red Cloud's knowledge, Deon repeated the stories to Allen, who wrote them down. Allen's efforts during the decade to interest an eastern book publisher in the manuscript came to nothing, and he turned to Sheldon, a former associate.

Sheldon received a typescript from Allen as early as 1902 and agreed to shepherd it through publication, a promise he never kept. The 1902 transcript, which has not survived, was retyped by Sandoz in 1932. Portions of Allen's 1893 handwritten manuscript appeared in an obscure South Dakota magazine in 1895–1896, however, and provide an invaluable comparison to the surviving document. Unfortunately, the whereabouts of Allen's original notes and manuscript are unknown today, but the details of the time, place, and persons involved in writing the "Life" are known and lend credibility to the surviving typed manuscript, annotated and published here under the title *Autobiography of Red Cloud*.

This title was chosen advisedly, for although Sheldon's involvement clouded the fact, "Life of Red Cloud" is more than a narrative biography. Rather, it is Red Cloud's *autobiography*, defined here as the story of one's own life written by oneself or dictated to another. Such an expansive definition is necessary when considering Native American autobiographies, a genre that has depended largely on narrators who did not speak English, interpreters of varied skill as cultural intermediaries, and white authors as often heavy-handed editors. As a result, some observers of the genre ignore entirely the distinctions between biography and autobiography, and in this instance that seems fair.

These considerations help address a problem that all of Charles Allen's potential publishers and modern historians encountering the document have faced, for the autobiography seemed to have lost its native voice and with it the opportunity to contribute significantly to our knowledge of Red Cloud's life. An examination of the history of Red Cloud's story and an understanding of Native American autobiography show otherwise.

Acknowledgments

SEVERAL INDIVIDUALS AIDED ME considerably in my search to recover Red Cloud's story. First and foremost were my colleagues at the Nebraska State Historical Society: Jim Potter of the Research and Publications Division and Cindy Drake and Marlene Roesler of the Library-Archives. Executive director Lawrence J. Sommer granted permission for the publication of the Red Cloud manuscript. Tom Buecker, curator of the Fort Robinson Museum and fellow gadabout, proved to be his usual supportive self.

Much appreciated archival assistance came from Mark Corriston and Mike Broadhead of the National Archives–Central Plains Region; Mark Hertig and Palma Wilson of the National Park Service; and Cindy Glum, Laura Glum, Marvene Riis, and Linda Sommer of the South Dakota State Historical Society. My thanks go to Dr. James C. Olson, who not only kindly responded to my inquiries but also kept meticulous research notes on Red Cloud, which he had earlier deposited with the Nebraska State Historical Society Archives.

John D. McDermott of Sheridan, Wyoming, commented on an earlier draft of the introduction; Jack also shared his considerable knowledge on the subject of Red

Cloud and his contemporaries. Charles Rankin and Marilyn Grant of the Montana Historical Society expertly shepherded to publication the article that preceded this book; to Martha Kohl of the Montana Historical Society and David Brumble of the University of Pittsburgh goes my gratitude for their valuable suggestions on how to expand and improve my introduction and annotation.

Two individuals served as needed sounding boards. Dick Jensen, an NSHS collaborator whose work with Charles Allen's autobiography paralleled my own with Red Cloud's, shared his thoughts, opinions, and research on this fascinating fellow. My many conversations with Bob Larson, who had retired from the University of Northern Colorado only to delve into a new biography of Red Cloud, were always enthusiastic and illuminating as we sought to understand this great man. I hope the three of us do justice to their life histories and help add to the ongoing pride of the Allen, Red Cloud, and Deon families.

The person who years ago set me on the trail of Red Cloud's autobiography was Jim Hanson, then director of the Nebraska State Historical Society. My first reaction to his innocent suggestion that I look at the document anew was an immediate snort of dismissal. I had concluded earlier—along with a couple of generations of historians—that the narrative was more fiction than fact, more Addison E. Sheldon than Red Cloud. Jim kept me digging until I started turning up clues that proved otherwise.

Finally and most important, I wish to acknowledge the assistance and encouragement of Lori Cox-Paul, my wife and fellow historian. She was immediately taken with the stories, always knew this was a worthwhile project, and diligently kept me at it. As Red Cloud once said admiringly of Pretty Owl, his wife, "She kept on my trail." To Lori I dedicate this book.

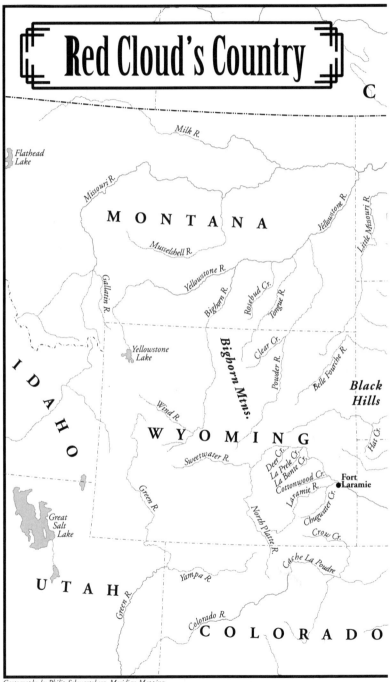

Red Cloud's Country

C

"I was born a Lakota and I have lived
as a Lakota and I shall die a Lakota."

—RED CLOUD, 1903
as quoted by Dr. James Walker

Editor's Introduction

AN OLD, BLIND MAN, Red Cloud needed the assistance of a family member in spring 1893 when he walked from his white frame house to the Pine Ridge, South Dakota, post office each day for his mail and some conversation. The Oglala Lakota warrior who had wiped out Captain William J. Fetterman's command, closed the Bozeman Trail, and brought the United States to a peace conference now needed the steady hand of a young relative to make the one-and-one-half-mile walk. Red Cloud received his mail from the Pine Ridge Agency postmaster, Charles Allen, who could boast of his political connections to the new Cleveland administration as well as to the Sioux tribe, having married an Oglala woman two decades before. Red Cloud often rendezvoused at the post office with Sam Deon, a French Canadian trader and his friend of forty years, and talked of the old days. Together, Red Cloud, Allen, and Deon, three veterans of the Old West, would collaborate on an extraordinary document—the autobiography of Chief Red Cloud.

A Long Career

WHAT A LIFE the old man had led, and imagine the stories he could tell! Achieving great success in his younger years as a Lakota warrior, Red Cloud became arguably his people's greatest war leader until the rise of Crazy Horse. Yet his early achievements, which garnered him so much acclaim and status among his Lakota peers, brought little, if any, attention in the historical record kept by whites. This changed when the middle-aged Red Cloud burst on the scene during the Bozeman War (1865–1868). Even so, the details of his early life and career, his ancestry, and his birth, all the facts near and dear to a biographer, remained a secondary concern to those chroniclers more interested in his later actions.

Red Cloud was born in 1821 along Blue Creek, a tributary of the North Platte River in present Garden County, Nebraska. His father, Lone Man, was a Brulé Lakota who had married a sister of the Oglala leader Smoke. Her name was Walks As She Thinks. Lone Man died while his son was but a small child, probably about 1825, and Smoke undoubtedly became Red Cloud's surrogate father and role model as a tribal leader.[1]

Smoke led the Bad Face band of the Oglalas, a group that, along with the Brulé division of the Lakotas and the other Oglala bands, served as the vanguard of Western Sioux expansion on the Great Plains. Their inexorable push from the east had brought Lakota groups to the rich buffalo ranges of the central plains and westward to the Rockies.[2] As Red Cloud observed in 1903: "We moved on our hunting grounds from the Minnesota to the Platte and from the Mississippi to the great mountains. No one put bounds about us."[3]

These were fluid times for the Lakotas. The 1820s

was a decade when relatively few whites lived in the West, and most of those who did were "mountain men," more interested in profits than permanent homes. The great wagon migrations were a quarter century away, and the Americans posed no immediate threat. The Lakota invasion west and south from the Missouri River, however, had brought them into conflict with several resident native groups, and stiff competition for the region's resources resulted in a brutal, decades-long struggle.[4]

The Lakotas forged alliances with the Cheyenne and Arapaho tribes, and together they pushed the Crows from the Black Hills to the Bighorn country in present Montana and Wyoming. There, Crow tribesmen warded off Lakota raids upon their lives and property. The Kiowas suffered similarly, and soon the Pawnees would abandon the rich bison ranges near the North and South Platte valleys of present western Nebraska for the comparative safety of the east. As illustrated by Red Cloud on a personal scale, the fortunes of war usually favored the Lakotas.

By the late 1840s the hunting range was split by a wagon road west, and the vast buffalo herds began to recede to territories heavily contested by the warring tribes. One historian has accurately noted the main goal of Lakota warfare for this time: "the invasion and safe hunting of disputed buffalo grounds without any cost to themselves."[5] Red Cloud became a singularly successful instrument in this policy.

It was only a matter of time before Lakota expansionism came into conflict with that other great power, the United States. The 1848 discovery of gold in California brought thousands of disruptive emigrants across Sioux land in 1849 and 1850. The government knew the situation could prove volatile and asked the Lakotas and other Plains tribes to a conference in 1851 to ease tensions and patch together an agreement. The Horse

Creek Treaty, sometimes called the Fort Laramie Treaty
of 1851, allowed for the safe passage of white travelers
along the trail, compensated the tribes for tolerating this
nuisance, prohibited warfare between the tribes, and established strict tribal boundaries. All parties largely ignored these last two elements.

Despite the treaty, tension mounted between the
Lakotas and the United States Army. First, near Fort
Laramie in 1854, Sioux warriors killed all of the soldiers
under Lieutenant John Grattan's command, after Grattan
and his troops marched into the Indians' camp to placate
the demands of a passing emigrant and opened fire. The
army retaliated in 1855 with the "battle" of Blue Water,
attacking a village of Brulés camped coincidentally at the
same stream along which Red Cloud was born. Red
Cloud, who witnessed the former event "where 30 were
killed," did not figure in the latter, nor did he attempt to
stem the tide of white emigration along the Platte Valley
route, which continued unabated in the 1850s. An un-
easy American-Lakota truce persisted during the decade.
In the case of Red Cloud, avoidance reduced the opportunity for direct conflict as his Bad Faces withdrew their
village to the Powder River country, one of their few remaining hunting paradises.[6]

In 1862 the situation changed drastically for the
Lakotas and for Red Cloud, now comfortably settled in
his role as "a big Chief."[7] Outside forces in the form of
gold discoveries in present Montana and yet another en-
suing rush of miners once again brought the competing
interests of nations into play, this time with far bloodier
results. The Bozeman Trail, named after the man who
blazed it, promised a more direct route to the goldfields;
however, users passed directly through the Lakota refuge in present north-central Wyoming and southeastern
Montana. This incursion into their prime, undisturbed

hunting grounds was intolerable. No longer could Red
Cloud, wisely chosen by the Oglalas to be their head
warrior, confine his attention to Indian enemies of the
Lakotas. War against the whites was unavoidable.[8]

Sporadic raids against white emigrants in 1863 were
followed a year later by a full-blown, concerted attack
by hundreds of allied Lakota, Cheyenne, and Arapaho
raiders along the length of the Platte Valley road. This
critical east-west transportation-communication lifeline
was for a time effectively cut. Not surprisingly, conditions were even worse for travelers on the more remote,
less protected Bozeman Trail. The United States Army,
its attention necessarily focused on defeating the South,
strived with its limited western garrisons to protect the
overlanders.

A major response against the Lakotas came with the
Powder River Expedition in 1865, after hostilities had
ceased on the eastern battlefields of the Civil War. When
three army columns under Patrick E. Connor invaded
the Powder River country in summer and fall 1865, they
failed to bring about a decisive engagement with Red
Cloud's warriors, but instead suffered unceasing harass-
ment. The expedition's commander settled on building
three soldier forts along the Bozeman Trail.[9]

Far from protecting the trail, the three outposts—
Forts Reno, Phil Kearny, and C. F. Smith—served as light-
ning rods, drawing the constant ire of the enraged Lakotas
and their allies. The remainder of the year and all the
next were marked by a virtually incessant state of war.
What the government could not achieve on the battlefield, it tried to accomplish at the bargaining table. In
June 1866 Red Cloud came to Fort Laramie to council,
but negotiations faltered, and both parties continued as
they had previously.

The Fetterman Massacre, Red Cloud's stunning

military victory against the United States Army, ended the political stalemate and made his reputation among whites. On December 21, 1866, Red Cloud's army lured Captain William J. Fetterman and the eighty men in his command away from the safety of the palisaded Fort Phil Kearny. Fetterman's troops were annihilated. Suddenly, after the Fetterman Massacre, the "Sioux problem" had a name associated with it—Red Cloud.

Soon a face accompanied the name. Now a recognized political leader, Red Cloud forced the government to negotiate—on Lakota terms. With masterful timing he dawdled and delayed his arrival to the great treaty council at Fort Laramie until November 1868, driving government representatives and the general public mad with apprehension. Ada Vogdes, a young army wife stationed at the fort, epitomized the mixed emotions that Red Cloud aroused. In one breath she called him one of the "worst Indians on the Plains," and in another calmly described him as "about six feet high and very quiet when spoken to. [He] has a pleasant smile, and no show or dash in any movement."[10]

When Red Cloud finally signed the peace accords, he could look upon his performance proudly. He had forced the abandonment of the hated trail through the Powder River country and the three forts that guarded it. He could not have known that he would be the only Indian leader to win a war against the United States or that this document would have such long-lasting ramifications for his people.[11]

The provisions of the Fort Laramie Treaty of 1868 did little, though, to ease strained relations, and in 1870, now a spokesman not only for his Oglalas but for the entire Lakota nation, Red Cloud journeyed to Washington to negotiate directly with President Ulysses S. Grant. As a consequence he became stunningly famous. The head-warrior-turned-statesman and his entourage took the country by storm. Newspapers recounted his every word and deed, and large crowds of onlookers gathered at every public sighting of the celebrated group. One Nebraska correspondent wrote breathlessly:

> The fame of Red Cloud, the Chief of the Sioux Nation, the most powerful band of savages on the American continent, is now world-wide, recent events having been of a nature which has lifted the warrior from the obscurity of the wigwams, the hunting grounds, and the war-paths of his forest home, and placed him high up in the list of the distinguished notables of the land. His name has been heralded with electric speed, within a month, to the remotest parts of the civilized world, and his position has made him in name, if not in reality, great.[12]

Red Cloud's own public statements were less baroque. He had come to Washington to be heard, and he was. But as he told the secretary of the interior: "I know I have been wronged. The words of my Great Father never reach me, and mine never reach him. There are too many streams between us."[13] For the remainder of his public life, Red Cloud would attempt to ford those streams. Red Cloud never generated the same level of public electricity for subsequent visits, but he continued to receive considerable notice each of the many times he journeyed to Washington. He made his last delegation trip in 1897.

Over three decades as an elder statesman, Red Cloud wrestled with the enormous problems that faced the Lakota nation. Those were years marked by the tortured transition of the free Lakota people to reservation life and punctuated by the immense conflicts of the Great Sioux War of 1876–1877 and the Ghost Dance troubles of 1890–1891. Other Lakota leaders, most notably Sitting Bull of the Hunkpapas, emulated Red Cloud's attempt at "deflecting the worst effects of white rule even while adapting to new ways of life." According to biographer Robert M. Utley, "[Sitting Bull] would be to the Hunkpapas what he imagined Red Cloud . . . to be to the Oglalas."[14]

To protect the remnants of his way of life, Red Cloud, ever the warrior, now drew from his culture a desperate tactic—the rearguard action. From experience and tradition he knew that, when retreating before an overwhelming enemy who threatened the people of his village, a Lakota warrior must valiantly attempt to slow or stop the enemy's advance, risking his own well-being to allow noncombatants the opportunity to escape to safety. Such altruism does not guarantee immediate success, much less later glory or appreciation, and Red Cloud's reputation has suffered accordingly. In fact, such desperate moves rarely turn the tide of battle, but they are some of the bravest acts a warrior can perform.

When Red Cloud died in 1909, his fight ended, the public remembered him primarily from his later years as a compromiser and emissary, not as a patriot warrior. His military accomplishments of a half century before were overshadowed by the more recent exploits of Crazy Horse, who conveniently died in his prime. Few could disagree, though, that Red Cloud's life writ large could serve as the nineteenth-century chronicle of the Oglala people.

The Red Cloud Narrative

BEFORE HE DIED, Red Cloud told a significant portion of his life history to Sam Deon, who in turn relayed it to Charles Allen to record for posterity. The history of the great man's personal narrative, the document itself, is a detective tale. It involves a healthy dose of deception, bad luck, bad faith, and erroneous judgments by scholars, which through the years transformed an important historical reference into a minor literary curiosity. New information, in the form of the private papers and diaries of Addison E. Sheldon, former superintendent of the Nebraska State Historical Society, should redeem the autobiography and perhaps qualify it for membership in an elite club. Only two American Indian leaders of Red Cloud's fame and stature—Black Hawk and Geronimo—left book-length, personal accounts of their lives.[15]

Their works, too, have been burdened by reader skepticism. According to the modern editor of *Black Hawk, an Autobiography*, "Since the first appearance of the autobiography in 1833, its accuracy, authenticity, and style have been both praised and damned." Also called into question has been the collaborative techniques employed by the editor of *Geronimo's Story of His Life*, who dismissed such criticisms rather brusquely: "The fact that Geronimo has told the story in his own way is doubtless the only excuse necessary to offer for the many unconventional features of this work."[16] Incredulity may be excused when one considers the agonizing ways in which these books and Red Cloud's narrative were created.

Charles Allen conceived the idea of writing Red Cloud's life history through surreptitiously interviewing Red Cloud to obtain the material for it and using Sam Deon as his clandestine intermediary. Allen explained the plan in a 1917 written statement taken by Addison E. Sheldon and preserved in Sheldon's personal papers (see Appendix B for a complete transcription of this document):

> The two used to put in two or three hours a day visiting on the bench by the post office, so I made arrangements with Mr. Deon to begin at the beginning and with questions and queries induced Red Cloud to

go over his life from the beginning. . . . Immediately at
the close of the conversation Mr. Deon would report to
me, and I would take down all the facts as notes. . . .
This continued through the whole summer and up to
late in the fall, practically six months in duration or until
the finish."[17]

According to Allen, Deon took up the narrative each
day where it had ended the day before. In this way Red
Cloud related memorable episodes of his life to Deon,
who repeated the stories to Allen. Allen then wrote them
down in note form in the same order as Red Cloud had
spoken them. This procedure is confirmed by Deon elsewhere: "Old Mr. Samuel Deon of Pine Ridge says that
he and Red Cloud were old friends and he used to go
and sit with him and talk over old times by the hour from
his birth up and then communicate what he had learned
to Postmaster Caufield [W. A. Coffield, Allen's assistant
in 1893, later Pine Ridge postmaster] and Chas. W. Allen
who wrote what they call his 'Life,' but this relates only
to his early life."[18]

Presumably Red Cloud, Deon, and Allen all had a
hand in assigning dates to the events Red Cloud described; unfortunately, their correspondence to other
historical sources often leaves much to be desired. Allen
remained silent on this (see Appendix B). Nevertheless,
the Red Cloud narrative ends rather abruptly and con-
clusively with the events of 1864. As Allen recalled: "Red
Cloud declined to tell the story of the rise of war with
the whites because he did not wish to revive those recollections. He claimed that they were past and that they
were friends with the whites."[19]

Red Cloud's reticence about aspects of his past was
long-standing. He often had refused to be "written up,"
wanting no part of a white man's money-making book

scheme.[20] His unwillingness may have stemmed from the
ill-mannered curiosity that whites usually displayed regarding his greatest achievement—winning a war against
the United States Army. Once accosted on a passenger
train and asked how many white men he had killed, Red
Cloud deftly replied through his interpreter, "Tell your
friend I have been in eighty battles."[21] As the years passed
and his physical and political powers diminished, Red
Cloud said even less to strangers. With his friends, however, the great chief thoroughly enjoyed reliving his glory
days and rise to power. He talked willingly about the years
before the white man's wars, before the Fetterman fight,
the days when he fought most of his "eighty battles."

Red Cloud's former national prominence assured him
of public attention for the remainder of his life, and, not
surprisingly, Allen sought to profit from this reservoir of
interest. Red Cloud, therefore, found two willing listeners at the Pine Ridge post office: Deon, who had seen
many of the later events Red Cloud described; and Allen,
who saw their commercial value if recorded and published.
Deon and Allen's joint effort created an autobiography
that is doubly special, both in the way it was told—confi-
dentially—and to whom it was told—from one longtime
friend to another. Contrast this to the more conventional
Black Hawk and Geronimo autobiographies, each a formal business arrangement between the Indian narrator
and a white associate, with a book as the ultimate goal.

No evidence exists that Red Cloud knew of Deon
and Allen's arrangement, nor is it known whether he
would have cared. After six months, Deon's methodical
probing may have aroused Red Cloud's suspicions, hence
the suspension of the old chief's storytelling when it
reached a more sensitive time in his life. Wittingly or not,
Red Cloud nonetheless helped sow the seeds for the
document's eventual dismissal. With the focus away from

the blood and thunder of the Bozeman Trail, Red Cloud's life did not particularly interest the public, and Allen was left with an unmarketable story, the narrative of America's greatest living Indian chief.

The disconcerting fact that the narrative does not read like a conventional autobiography created additional marketing difficulties. Red Cloud's political biographer, James C. Olson, observed accurately that the document's main problem is its language.[22] As the narrative wended its way from Red Cloud to Deon to Allen, what began in the first person ended in the third, probably because Deon rendered Red Cloud's words in the third person to Allen, who dutifully copied them down. Allen, a hopeful author to be, here made a tactical error. Use of the third person departed drastically from the more common "as-told-to" format of Native American autobiographies. Traditionally, white editors polished these works to make readers assume the words flowed unaltered from the mouths of their Indian narrators, with the virtually invisible editor playing the role of interested yet passive transcriber. One need only examine the history and popularity of *Black Elk Speaks* (1932), the best-known American Indian autobiography, to sense the magnitude of Allen's mistake with the Red Cloud narrative.[23]

While Allen's motives may have been purely exploitative, Sam Deon's were not. Deon was Red Cloud's friend, maybe his closest friend, and he does not seem to have benefited materially from the project. Although Deon's intentions on that post office bench in 1893 can be called into question, his demeanor differed little from that which he displayed on countless other occasions when the two men reflected on their many years together. Deon probably enjoyed the reminiscing as much as his friend, hence his prominent role in some of the later stories.

Both Deon and Allen were eminently qualified to

interview Red Cloud. Samuel Deon had lived among the Lakotas since the 1850s.[24] A French Canadian from Montreal, Deon emigrated to Boston in his early twenties to join his two brothers and find work. That same year, 1847, he accompanied his Boston employer's shipload of ice to New Orleans. From New Orleans Deon continued upriver to St. Louis, where he hired on with the American Fur Company. Joining a crew destined for the company's upper Missouri trading posts, Deon wintered twenty miles from Fort Benton, present Montana, at an American Fur Company lumber camp. He returned to St. Louis the following year. In 1851 he again joined the American Fur Company for another trip up the Missouri, serving as a valet of sorts to Father Pierre-Jean De Smet, S.J.

Deon served the company and its successors many years as an Indian trader among the Lakotas. He took goods to their winter camps and returned to his employer in the spring with robes and furs. He became fluent in their language, and, following the custom of the day, took as his wife a woman from the tribe. He lived with Red Cloud who became his sponsor, protector, and friend.[25]

Except for the facts found in this narrative, little is known of Deon's life among the Indians, although his association with the Oglala Lakotas spans decades. He hung around the Fort Laramie area for years. In the 1860 United States Census of the Fort Laramie area he is enumerated as "Samuel Dun," a thirty-five-year-old clerk for trader William F. Lee. Other records show Deon in the employ of Lee's brother-in-law Geminien P. Beauvais. After leaving Red Cloud's camp before war broke out, Deon suffered the loss of several hundred dollars' worth of horses stolen by Sioux raiders in October 1864. On June 14, 1865, he happened to be present at the Horse Creek fight east of Fort Laramie when Indians, unwilling to be taken to Fort Kearny, Nebraska Territory, escaped from their military escort, killing Captain William D. Fouts in the process.[26] These setbacks notwithstanding, Eugene Ware, another army officer of the time, described "Sam Dion" as "one of the pioneer Frenchman of the period, a jolly, royal, generous fellow who cared for nothing particularly, was happy everywhere, and whom the very fact of existence filled with exuberance and joy."[27]

Later, Deon's name graced the list of witnesses to the Fort Laramie Treaty of 1868. On an 1891 affidavit Deon claimed that he had been a resident of the reservation for twenty-one years, indicating that he may have followed the Oglalas from their first agency on the North Platte River in 1871 to the new Red Cloud Agency on the White River in 1873. His Oglala wife and four children were listed as residing in the village of American Horse at Red Cloud Agency in early 1877. Deon probably moved with the tribe to the Missouri River in the winter of 1877–1878 and finally to Pine Ridge later in 1878.[28]

For Allen's purposes, Deon, who also possessed a good command of the English language, was an ideal translator and partner. Allen had a background as a newspaperman; together they made a formidable pair of amateur historians.

Like Deon, Charles Wesley Allen was an experienced westerner.[29] Born in Noble County, Indiana, on September 10, 1851, he, too, worked his way west as a young man. Arriving at Mankato, Kansas, he joined the state militia in 1869 and guarded the western Kansas frontier from marauders. In June 1871 he signed on as a trail hand to herd cattle to Cheyenne, Wyoming Territory, and after his arrival found a job on a stock ranch west of Fort Laramie. He remained in southeastern Wyoming for a decade, ranching and occasionally working as a Black Hills freighter.

On August 23, 1873, Allen married Emma Hawkins,

the mixed-blood Lakota daughter of Henry Hockenstriser, or Hochstrasser (anglicized to Hawkins), and the granddaughter of Joseph Bissonette, a longtime trader in the Fort Laramie area. Charles and Emma raised a large family that by 1896 numbered five daughters and four sons.[30]

In 1881 Allen moved his brood to the Pine Ridge country of Dakota Territory. He helped build government buildings, freighted between the Missouri River and the Pine Ridge and Rosebud reservations, and two years later moved to Valentine, Nebraska, where he edited a newspaper called the *Democrat*. In 1885 he founded the Chadron *Democrat* in the new town of Chadron, Nebraska. Allen's most noteworthy story during his career as a newspaperman was his eyewitness account of the 1890 fight at Wounded Knee Creek and the massacre of Big Foot's village.[31] In 1893, fellow Democrat and newly elected President Grover Cleveland appointed Allen as the postmaster for Pine Ridge, South Dakota.[32] By then, Charles W. Allen had been intimately associated with Red Cloud's Oglalas for twenty years.

Despite Allen and Deon's well-planned, well-executed efforts, the manuscript they produced languished for one hundred years, virtually unknown. The work was first mentioned in a Chadron newspaper in December 1893, with the following postscript: "Charlie has already received several flattering offers for it from eastern publishing houses."[33] Contrary to this report, Allen apparently had trouble finding a publisher for the manuscript.

Portions of it appeared in 1895 and 1896 in *The Hesperian*, a short-lived literary magazine published by Kenneth F. Harris in Hot Springs, South Dakota. Harris, who later wrote regularly for the *Saturday Evening Post*, was one of many individuals who may have left their mark on the autobiography. Only five issues of his little magazine are known to exist, and three contain Allen excerpts.

Allen, who may have had some financial interest in the magazine, prepared three installments. Titled "Red Cloud, Chief of the Sioux," the series used the first fourth of the entire autobiography (chapters 1 through 6 of this volume).[34]

Allen next contacted Warren K. Moorehead, a pioneering archaeologist for the Ohio State Archaeological and Historical Society and later for the Phillips Academy of Andover, Massachusetts. Moorehead, who also served for twenty-six years as a member of the United States Board of Indian Commissioners, knew Allen from their days as newspaper correspondents covering the 1890 Ghost Dance disturbance on the Pine Ridge Reservation.[35] From Allen, Moorehead received an original handwritten manuscript and had it typed. He returned both copies to Allen, who proofread the typescript.[36] Although Moorehead praised Allen's work and subsequently used data from the manuscript in his own work, *The American Indian in the United States* (1914), his general lack of enthusiasm for the manuscript foreshadowed the lackluster reaction of other scholars.[37] Because the narrative dealt little with events deemed important to the winning of the West, the focus of most studies then and since, it could play but a minor role as a historical reference.

When Moorehead proved little help in finding a publisher, Allen turned to Addison E. Sheldon, another old colleague. He sent a typed copy of the manuscript to Sheldon, a former newspaperman from Allen's Chadron days and a onetime friendly rival. Sheldon had edited another newspaper in Chadron, where he often suffered from Allen's mocking editorials criticizing Sheldon's views on populism and temperance. By the 1900s, Sheldon was a noted Nebraska historian employed by the state historical society in Lincoln and a statehouse politician. He had won election as a representative to the Nebraska legislature in 1896, and his fortunes were rising. The same could not be said for Allen, who no longer held his position as Pine Ridge postmaster and apparently was experiencing limited success as a rancher on the Little White River, present Bennett County, South Dakota.

Sheldon and Allen met at the Nebraska border town of Merriman, the nearest railway point to the latter's ranch, on December 23, 1902, and decided to edit and publish Allen's work jointly. As Sheldon wrote in his diary that day: "He [Allen] is to turn over to me all his Mss and data of every kind and assist in securing other data. I am to do all the preparations and publishing, to be sent out under our joint names and equal division of proceeds."[38] It was a fateful—and unlucky—day for Allen. For forty years Sheldon would do little if anything with the manuscript, then titled "Life of Red Cloud."

A Document "Lost"

ADDISON E. SHELDON kept personal diaries for almost four decades. In 1953 the diaries came to the Nebraska State Historical Society, Lincoln, from Ruth Sheldon, his daughter, but were closed to researchers at her insistence for twenty-five years. They tell a fitful, frustrating story. Together with Sheldon's official correspondence to Allen and a number of other people during his tenure as superintendent of the Nebraska State Historical Society (1917–1943), the diaries show that Sheldon worked on the manuscript occasionally but that his grandiose plans for a massive, comprehensive biography of Red Cloud and the history of the Sioux nation, with the Allen manuscript as its cornerstone, never materialized.

After meeting with Allen in December 1902, Sheldon proceeded immediately to Pine Ridge, where he met and interviewed Sam Deon and Postmaster W. A. Coffield,

Allen's former assistant who had transcribed in ink Allen's penciled notes. Although Sheldon's trip to Pine Ridge was hurried, he tried, with Deon along, to call on Red Cloud, but the old chief was away from home.[39]

Sheldon returned to Pine Ridge on June 15, 1903, and, again with Deon, interviewed Red Cloud on the three following days. Deon then vanishes from the story. At best a shadowy figure in the historical record, Deon's subsequent involvement with the Red Cloud manuscript remains unknown.

Red Cloud the storyteller had deteriorated markedly in the intervening decade, or so Sheldon concluded. Learning nothing from Allen and Deon's technique, Sheldon came away with little from the feeble chief except for Red Cloud's brief statement about one war exploit—"First time I went to war with Crows I stole two horses. That was long time ago"—and a denial of being in the Fetterman fight.[40]

Turning from oral history, Sheldon gathered documentary references to Red Cloud and Indian-white relations but produced no written narrative. Except for passing mention in his diary, Sheldon seems to have dropped the subject entirely, or at least until Red Cloud died in 1909, when he penned a long exposition for a Lincoln newspaper. He also made an overture to James H. Cook, another long-standing friend of Red Cloud and owner of the fossil-rich Agate Springs Ranch on the Niobrara River in Nebraska, for manuscript material on the Lakota chief. Cook wisely avoided Sheldon and a few years later published his own autobiography of frontier experiences, in which Red Cloud figures prominently. In fact, until now historians generally agreed that Cook's *Fifty Years on the Old Frontier* (1923) was "the closest thing that twentieth-century readers can get to a first-person account from Red Cloud."[41]

Evidence of a continued Allen-Sheldon partnership is meager. In 1908 Sheldon saw Allen in Lincoln where, Sheldon said, they "talked the old times." Sheldon coldly added: "He is candidate for an oil inspectorship—with no chance—is broke—sad case."[42] In 1915 Sheldon wrote to inform Allen, now the editor of the Martin, South Dakota, *Messenger*, that he had gathered "a large mass of material" but realized that "the long delay in producing the final result is a grief to us both."[43] The two met again in 1917, when Sheldon recorded Allen's description of how Deon interviewed Red Cloud in 1893 and how Deon then translated the narrative to Allen, but Sheldon did nothing further.

The years of inaction must have weighed heavily on Allen because he solicited the help of others to break the logjam in Lincoln. Once again Allen called on his friend Moorehead, who passed on the request to E. A. Brininstool, a noted western historian and collector living in Los Angeles, who, in turn, wrote Cook at his ranch. Brininstool and Sheldon were collaborating cordially on an issue of *Nebraska History* devoted to Crazy Horse, but Brininstool's comments to Cook reveal the jealousies among historians of the day. The letter reads in part:

> Well begorry, will you just read all the enclosed letters! Take them just as I have them arranged, and you will see that maybe old man Sheldon has been swiping something he has no business to own. It sure looks that way from Allen's letter and statement.
>
> It is quite apparent that Moorehead wants us to help him get hold of that Red Cloud MSS from Sheldon. After all these years—Allen don't say WHEN he gave it to him, but over 20 years ago—it may be a hard matter to get Sheldon to "come thru" with the stuff. Nobody knows its value of course, but you can bet

that Moorehead would not have tackled it if it had
not been of great value—and he ought to know. . . .
Moorehead don't say that he is going to write Sheldon,
so it may be he is waiting to hear from me as to a course
of action. [The previous sentence is crossed out. Written above is "I see he has written him."] Maybe you
better write Moorehead direct. . . . I believe you said
you knew of this man Allen. Do you know if he is reliable, and really has some valuable stuff that Red Cloud
himself gave him? . . . How does all this strike you?[44]

How all this struck Cook is unknown because no follow-
up letters between Sheldon, Cook, Brininstool, or
Moorehead are available. Indeed, not until the 1930s did
Sheldon's interest in the book revive. In October 1931
he again sought to entice manuscript materials from Cook;
once more Cook did not respond.[45]

Then, on February 15, 1932, Sheldon wrote in his
diary: "Red Cloud Mss—found. It has been lost several
years. Set Miss Mari Sandoz at work typing it for use in
my own Red Cloud life." Mari Sandoz took to the task
in her capacity as a paid employee of the Nebraska State
Historical Society who was assisting Sheldon in his research.
While typing the manuscript for Sheldon, Sandoz was also
working on *Old Jules*, the prizewinning biography of her
father, which three years later would catapult her into the
front ranks of western writers.[46] When she completed her
typing, Sandoz had produced the manuscript that survives
today. Sheldon mentions Allen's efforts in his introduction to the manuscript, but its title, "Life of Red Cloud by
Addison E. Sheldon," and his diary entry betray whom he
believed the "author" for any biography would be. The
distinctions between Sheldon's and Allen's contributions,
meanwhile, had become increasingly hazy.

Sheldon, by then in his seventies, commissioned a
Washington researcher to gather more documents at the

National Archives. He also corresponded with Allen, whose fortunes had declined steadily in the intervening years. Allen's wife Emma had died in 1924, and he resided in the state soldiers home in Hot Springs, South Dakota. Allen's hopes may have been buoyed briefly because work on the Red Cloud biography consumed Sheldon for several months, during which time his documentary collections on Sioux history grew to fill several file cabinets. All of Sheldon's renewed activity ended abruptly, however, and the Red Cloud narrative was again put aside as more pressing matters engaged Sheldon's time. Sheldon's planned "Life of Red Cloud" and his stranglehold on Allen's manuscript ended with his long illness and death in 1943.

Charles Allen had died a year earlier in 1942, but not before he tried to get *his* autobiography published. In 1938, still residing in the soldiers home in Hot Springs, Allen finished a 298-page memoir titled, "In the West That Was." Incredibly, Allen sent the manuscript to Sheldon, who, not surprisingly, failed to find him a publisher.[47] Allen also shared his autobiography with Elmo Scott Watson, a journalism professor at Northwestern University, member of the Chicago Westerners, and editor of *Publisher's Auxiliary*, a trade journal for newspaper publishers. Watson published a few excerpts from Allen's autobiography about the Ghost Dance troubles at Pine Ridge Reservation in 1890–1891 in *Publisher's Auxiliary*, and these were later reprinted.[48]

Sheldon's successor as superintendent of the Nebraska State Historical Society was James C. Olson, who partially fulfilled Sheldon's dream. Olson expanded on Sheldon's Red Cloud research, brought a professional approach to the subject, and, after leaving the historical society, produced *Red Cloud and the Sioux Problem* (1965). Olson's book detailed relations between the Lakotas and the federal government, with Red Cloud's political career as its centerpiece. Such a focus did not depend on expansive detail about Red Cloud's early years, although Olson cited the Red Cloud manuscript several times.[49] Olson's book, in turn, complemented George E. Hyde's *Red Cloud's Folk* (1937), a history of the Oglala Sioux. Hyde, an Omaha, Nebraska, historian and author of later, similar studies on the Brulé Sioux and Pawnees, had known of Sheldon's prior claim to the subject but proceeded with his own work nonetheless. Sheldon's reputation for dawdling was well known.

On the other hand, Sheldon successfully hid the Allen manuscript from Hyde and from Walter S. Campbell, another historian of the Sioux, who wrote under the name Stanley Vestal.[50] Unaware of the information in Sheldon's private papers, Olson and others understandably gave Sheldon far more credit for the manuscript than he deserved. The Sheldon stigma, Allen's lost authorship, and the disconcerting use of the third-person voice in the narrative were enough to discredit the manuscript in the eyes of most historians, but it was Sandoz and her vitriol toward Red Cloud, the man, that consigned the manuscript to purgatory.

After resigning from the Nebraska State Historical Society in 1935, Sandoz wrote two novels, *Slogum House* (1937) and *Capital City* (1939), both commercial disappointments. Her next effort, *Crazy Horse: The Strange Man of the Oglalas* (1942), is what many consider her most important work. Often mistaken for nonfiction, Sandoz's *Crazy Horse* is a historical novel. It is what one eminent historian recently described as "good literature and bad history" and, as such, probably did more to damage Red Cloud's reputation than any work in print.[51] Sandoz, of course, was intimately acquainted with the contents of Red Cloud's autobiography, yet she ignored its flattering self-portrait, although she used at least one incident from the manuscript in her book. A ten-page fragment of the Red Cloud narrative, with the handwritten title "R.C. auto bio," perhaps assigned by Sandoz and covering an episode retold in *Crazy Horse*, resides in her personal papers.[52]

Sandoz's heroic Crazy Horse needed appropriate villains, and Red Cloud and his relatives were cast as such throughout her book. In Sandoz's story, Red Cloud was "reaching," a man whose actions were carried out "slyly" and "cunningly," who spoke with "a different wind out of each corner of the mouth," and who "seemed to be working for the white man."[53] Red Cloud's all-too-human attributes of pride, ambition, arrogance, and self-interest, readily apparent in the stories he chose to tell Deon, mutate in Sandoz's telling. In *Crazy Horse*, Red Cloud becomes a power-hungry, jealous adversary. This image of Red Cloud persists in the popular imagination and helps explain why Red Cloud has not been awarded the acclaim given Crazy Horse, who succeeded him as "the greatest of the fighting Oglalas."[54] Nor has it helped Red Cloud's reputation that most of his fights were against other Native Americans rather than against a horde of reminiscence-writing army officers. Perhaps the publication of this narrative will begin to restore Red Cloud's reputation.

The War Exploit and Native American Autobiography

THE ROLE OF WARFARE between the Lakotas and other Plains tribes provides the anthropological context for Red Cloud's life and career. War and trade gave the Lakotas access to horses and firearms, the acquisition of which directly affected their ability to engage offensively against their competitors and to follow their implicit policy of security through aggression.[55] But purely economic and political motives do not entirely explain the incentive for war. Red Cloud and his tribesmen's reasons for fighting also included more demonstrable personal rewards. Individual accomplishments in the fields of war and horse stealing provided Lakota men like Red Cloud the opportunity for social advancement. War prowess, so vital to the Lakotas' well-being, was individually the "surest avenue to renown," and it established Red Cloud's reputation and advanced his career along with those of other Sioux leaders.[56]

Red Cloud's own words show that the way to increase one's social standing was no mystery to this most talented practitioner: "When I was young among our nation, I was poor, but from wars with one nation and another I raised myself to be a chief."[57] But this statement and others like it provide few details on how he accomplished his rise to power. Scholars have written much about Plains warfare, but the particulars—firsthand sources on Lakota warfare by the participants—have been hard to uncover.[58] Red Cloud's may be one of the most informative Indian autobiographies on the subject of intertribal warfare.

The narrative's emphasis on Red Cloud's war exploits is not accidental. To translate military prowess into increased status, Red Cloud and his fellow warriors needed an effective means to link their distant deeds to peer recognition, and that device was the public recounting of their exploits. War honors were not only to be earned but to be corroborated, shared, and celebrated.[59] Looked upon from outside the culture, especially by nineteenth-century government representatives, such formal presentations seemed excessively boastful and irrelevant to the matters at hand. To the Lakotas, however, such autobiographical vignettes served a preliminary, yet necessary, function: To know a man's past achievements helped one to understand and respect his current place in society.

Red Cloud's emphasis on his military accomplishments, then, fits a Lakota cultural pattern and substantiates the narrative's authenticity. The question of authenticity has been at the center of my efforts to "recover" Red Cloud's autobiography. After tracing the document's torturous history, it became clear to me that the document was, in fact, Red Cloud's story. But the autobiography also appears authentic in the literary sense: *Red Cloud is in it*. He contributed meaningfully; he chose the topics and tells what was important to him. This follows the usual pattern of Native American as-told-to works, for which the narrator determined the subjects to be covered, although not necessarily the form they would take in the final manuscript. Such collaborations resulted in a mixed form, a strange creature of two cultures, that blur our traditional and seemingly inviolate distinctions between autobiography and biography.[60]

The genre of Native American autobiography, a fascinating and significant category of American literature, provides the literary context for Red Cloud's story.[61] Such works have been the subject of intense, comparative, scholarly scrutiny only recently, and they are still best understood in terms of their inherent limitations and largely untapped potential.[62]

Within the genre the Red Cloud document neatly falls into the category of a collaboration under the guise of history. Typically, an amateur became interested in those natives who had "made history," especially those who had resisted whites on the battlefield. Black Hawk's and Geronimo's autobiographies fit here, as do well-known works by Joseph White Bull and Wooden Leg, Lakota and Cheyenne warriors who fought at the Little Bighorn, and Yellow Wolf, a Nez Perce confederate of Chief Joseph. Their editors believed they were salvaging important stories and making serious contributions to the historical record.[63]

What is critical to such autobiographies is the presence of an Indian voice, in this case, Red Cloud's. Clearly one must look past the jarring choices of inappropriate terms found scattered throughout the narrative's pages. When one reads such ethnocentric words as "savages" (pages 32, 66, 183), "aboriginal" (page 108), "barbarous" (pages 73,150), "fiends" (page 127), and "high priest" (page 110), one is reading Charles Allen, the intrusive editor, and his choices of terminology then widely used, not the spoken words of Red Cloud.

The flesh-and-blood Lakota chief depicted in this narrative, however, still emerges through Allen's veil. He displays a much different persona than the older Red Cloud most whites came to know. The later image of Red Cloud is that of a weak, accommodating politician— reinforced by a procession of unflattering photographic portraits in his old age—who willingly chose the path of appeasement in exchange for fleeting power. True or not, this image deviates dramatically from the profile presented in the autobiography, that of a younger, vigorous Red Cloud, a fierce warrior and bold leader.

Red Cloud's narrative exhibits other features common to the genre. For example, Indian narrators often avoided recent, reservation-era events and focused, instead, on brief accounts of their war exploits. The stories of Plenty-coups, another excellent example from the published literature, illustrate both features from a Crow Indian perspective. He recounted several war exploits to his white editor, but "Plenty-coups refused to speak of his life after the passing of the buffalo, so that his story seems to have been broken off, leaving many years unaccounted for."[64]

As one scholar has observed, "It would never have occurred to these people to sit down and tell the story of their lives whole." By contrast, a white autobiographer would have presented his own life rather seamlessly, from formative youth to climactic pinnacle, occasionally inserting dramatic "turning points." Such features were foreign to a literature based on preliterate, oral, autobiographical traditions. In fact, one can assume that the more "unified" the autobiography, the more influential the editor.[65] That Red Cloud's stories retain their "shape" in the form of episodic, somewhat disconnected tales of adult achievements may indicate a faithfulness to their original telling not readily apparent or appreciated by later readers.

A second question concerning the Red Cloud manuscript remains elusive: is it *accurate?* Donald Jackson, who edited a later edition of Black Hawk's autobiography, addressed the authenticity and accuracy of that document in reverse order to my approach with the Red Cloud narrative. Jackson wrote in his introduction: "The accuracy we may test by checking with contemporary documents; the authenticity—the genuineness of the book as an utterance of Black Hawk—is harder to determine."[66] Red Cloud, on the other hand, has given us descriptions of intertribal encounters, told as long as a half century after they occurred, for which few contemporary documents exist. Corroboration from other eyewitnesses or from the oral histories of neighboring tribes may always be lacking, making efforts at further annotation daunting. Add the self-serving nature of any autobiography, especially when recounted through the rose-colored glasses of old age, and the manuscript's accuracy as an ethnohistorical document may suffer. Therefore, it is clear *what this document is not—* it is not an exhaustive life history. The narrative will never stand as the last word on the events preceding "Red Cloud's War," nor significantly illuminate the events of the war itself, and that may disappoint some students of the Indian wars. However, Allen realistically and accurately called this work "the Indian part of the life of Red Cloud," not a history of his people or of Indian-white relations.

Nevertheless, Red Cloud's autobiography should no longer be ignored, for it certainly adds to our understanding of the life of a notable individual and provides rare firsthand information about Plains warfare and Lakota warrior culture. It also offers the promise, though with limitations, of new information on previously undocumented events of importance to several tribal histories.

The inquiries of most historians of Charles Allen's generation only focused on shoot-'em-up Indian-white conflict. Their failure to investigate other, earlier aspects of Native American history makes the effort of Charles Allen and Sam Deon all the more laudable, for we may never get closer to Red Cloud. This modern edition of the great warrior's autobiography allows the old man to speak to us again, as he once spoke to Sam Deon on that bench in front of the Pine Ridge post office.

1

The Coming Chief

THE FIRST OF RED CLOUD'S stories begins with a mercifully short section devoted to background information on the "great Siouan family." These passages are undoubtedly Charles W. Allen's contribution, necessary, he felt, for Red Cloud's proper introduction to the reader. Red Cloud's people, their history, and ethnology were still ciphers to most Americans, even though their conflicts with the United States had consumed nearly a half century. In the 1890s the readily available scholarly readings on Lakota (Allen's "Dakotas or Sioux branch") history and ethnology were limited but rapidly growing. For example, linguist James Owen Dorsey had written several pioneering studies for the Smithsonian Institution and other learned bodies on "Siouan family" sociology, statements that Allen seems to have mimicked.[1]

Red Cloud, on the other hand, quickly enters the core of his narrative, apparently propelling straightaway to his earliest war exploit and past his childhood. Students of Native American autobiography will not find this surprising, but to other readers, used to less precipitous prologues, it may seem unexpectedly abrupt, even disquieting. One would hardly expect to pick up the autobiography of a comparable nineteenth-century American national figure, say the 1885 account penned by former President Ulysses S. Grant, and see his entire childhood skipped. Grant did not begin his memoirs as a young adult on his first Mexican War battlefield; he dutifully recorded his ancestry, birth, and boyhood in one chapter, followed by another on his formative years of training at West Point.[2]

Grant's Oglala counterpart—and his 1870 guest to the White House—followed a different model, one shared by other Native American contemporaries. Red Cloud wasted little breath on context—did Sam Deon, who had lived for four decades with his people, really need such information?—and moved into his first personal exploit. As Allen termed it and as Red Cloud probably perceived it himself, "[His] childhood days were passed in a manner common to all Indian children." It was during young adulthood, as told in this first story, that his promise as a future great leader became apparent.

It was appropriate that the first war party the sixteen year old accompanied was against the Pawnee tribe. When the events of this first story took place (about 1837–1838), the Lakotas were waging a brutal war of attrition against the Pawnees of east-central Nebraska, and raids against the earthlodge villages situated along the Platte River and its tributaries were common occurrences.[3] Accounts such as Red Cloud's provide an intimate—and surprisingly rare—glimpse at a budding warrior's life, a necessary complement to the broadbrush studies of the larger intertribal struggle.

On the banks of Blue Creek, near where its waters empty into the Platte River, opposite the mouth of Ash Hollow, where General Harney made his famous fight against the Sioux in 1855, in what is now Deuel County, Nebraska, Red Cloud, the subject of this biography was born in May 1821. He belongs to what is termed the Bad Face band, a small subdivision of Oglalas who are a numerically strong subdivision of the Dakotas, constituting the greater part of the western division of the great Siouan family, whose territory once extended from near the Saskatchewan River in the British possessions, southward, embracing both Dakotas, the greater part of Montana, part of Wyoming, nearly all of Iowa, Nebraska, Kansas, Missouri, Arkansas, and Indian Territory, and extending east from the Dakotas, including a large part of Minnesota and Wisconsin as far as the shore of Lake Michigan. They had also a small possession on the north shore of the Gulf of Mexico in Mississippi, and another strip of territory extending through the Carolinas and Virginia into Maryland as far as the Potomac River.

Such were the ancient possessions of the Dakotas, Crows, Poncas, Osages, Kaws, Quapaws, Otoes, Biloxi, and Catauba and many other tribes that had been grouped on account of linguistic relationship, as the great Siouan family.

The Dakotas or Sioux branch of the family still have their abiding place upon different reservations mostly within the limits of the states of North and South Dakota, and the greater number of these Indians are located on the Rosebud and Pine Ridge reservations along the southern boundaries of South Dakota. It is here that one can see the Sioux in various grades of civilization, from the comfortable, down the scale to the poor and dirty savages, or again, warriors dressed in all the gaudiness of their pristine splendor—as you like. It is at Pine Ridge, the largest Indian agency in the United States, that Red Cloud lives. He has lived there continually ever since the establishment of the agency in 1879 and can be seen almost every day coming to the agency for his mail. He is always dressed in citizen's clothes and nearly always carries a cane, although his step is firm and elastic and his carriage straight; age is telling on him of course, but most particularly is it noticeable in his failing eyesight which necessitates the use of glasses continually.

Red Cloud has never been considered a great orator by his people; there have always been a number of Indians among them that excelled him in this respect, and he always availed himself of the services of such as these, in the capacity of head men, subchiefs, etc., and largely through these orators have his thoughts and plans been conveyed to the multitude.

Being a man of strong reasoning power, great determination and honesty of purpose, and not having been born a chief, but having raised himself to that position by the judicious exercise of a laudable but never slumbering ambition, he has never, during the long term of his chieftaincy, suffered any encroachment by his tribe on his imperial right to rule, and the conclusion of no council of importance has ever been considered as final until Red Cloud's opinion and consent were had. Even now, although he has lost much of his martial bearing, and is declining in health, under the weight of years, and though religious fanaticisms of the Ghost Dance order have rent his people into factions and though the policy of the government is fast undermining the systems and customs in vogue under tribal relations, Red Cloud's counsel is sought and valued by all the subchiefs and head men of the tribe, and he enjoys the confidence and respect of all.

Red Cloud has often incurred the displeasure of treaty commissions and sometimes of Indian agents and has been termed by them as "hard headed," yet he always stood for what he deemed was right and could not be swayed. If he thought a special treaty was to the advantage of his people, he boldly espoused its consummation; if on the contrary, after due deliberation, he thought that it appeared unjust or unfair, he boldly though often hopelessly opposed it.

But it is not the purpose of the writer to treat of Red Cloud's treaties, speeches, and semi-official acts with the Indian department; these are all a matter of record. This is simply a story of the Indian part of the life of Red Cloud, who stands today without a peer among the living aboriginal chieftains, and who, when antiquity shall have lent its charm to his name and prowess, will take his place in the galaxy of the great Indian chiefs of America.

The different Sioux bands at the time of which I speak occupied a large scope of country extending from the British line on the north to the Arkansas River on the south, over which they roamed, having their villages located at different points from time to time as inclination or necessity directed. Rarely were their camps maintained in one place to exceed two months, except in winter, and then only when an exceptionally favored spot had been selected. The reason for this is obvious; by moving they would naturally get nearer to game that would naturally drift away from the country immediately surrounding their camp. They could also get fresh pastures for their ponies, and find wood more easily attainable in a new camp.

It was in these movable villages that Red Cloud's childhood days were passed in a manner common to all Indian children. His father, whose name was Red Cloud, as was also his grandfather's, had died a few months before the present Red Cloud was born, and the name which seems to have been one peculiar to this family was given to his cousin, a lad some ten years his senior who bore it until he was killed in an engagement with the Pawnees when twenty-six years old.

At this time the coming chief was sixteen years of age and the Oglala Sioux were camped on the North Platte, north of old Fort Laramie, in what is now Wyoming. Soon after the return of the party of warriors who had been out against the Pawnees, and among whom Red Cloud's cousin had been numbered, and slain, another war party of increased numbers was organized and another raid against the Pawnees planned. Red Cloud joined this party much against the wishes of his mother who tried in every way to dissuade him from taking such a hazardous journey.

Her persistence in objecting was so well understood throughout the village that when the young warriors congregated at a given place preparatory to starting, the absence of the young man was quickly noted, and immediately attributed to his "heart having failed him." Much sport was being indulged in at his expense as the party started, when a shout arose from among the bystanding women, "He is coming."

"Who is coming?"

Then it seems to have occurred to the people of the village that the young man was without a name, when someone answered "Red Cloud's son." "Red Cloud!" shouted another, and then the shout became general. "Red Cloud comes, Red Cloud comes!" and the young man dashed up, mounted upon a fine spotted horse decked with all the paint and feathers that belong to a warrior's equipment, leading a splendid bay. Amid shouts of congratulations he joined the party having thus ridden to his name and the beginning of the realization of his long cherished dream of the "pomp and circumstance of glorious war."

The party followed down the North Platte River to its junction with the South Platte and then continued its course down the north side of the main stream to within a few days travel of where Fort Kearney was afterwards established, in what is now Kearney County, Nebraska. Here the forerunners had located the Pawnee village and the Sioux made a detour through the hills approaching the village en masse, shooting into their lodges and yelling their war cry.

The startled Pawnees sprang from their beds armed with bows and arrows, clubs and guns and engaged the Sioux in a hand to hand conflict, but the latter being mounted could wield their war clubs with deadly effect.

They dashed over women and children, striking them to the ground by the force of their running horses and were fast nearing the side of the village opposite to where they entered and were about to turn and dash through the edge of the village where the defense was weaker, when they were suddenly confronted by a large body of Pawnees who came up over a small hill that lay between the main village and a small creek that runs into the Platte from the north.

The Sioux had a good understanding of the location of the Pawnee camp, having previously sent their scouts to reconnoitre, but the fact dawned upon them that the creek beyond the hill was skirted by a large number of Pawnee lodges that had been moved there after dark and therefore were not taken into account by their scouts. Acting on this impression, which proved to be correct, they turned and made a fighting retreat up to the bluff, where they scattered, splitting into parties of four or five, each party gathering up as many of the Pawnees' horses as possible.

When they met at the rendezvous about forty miles from the Pawnee village up the Platte River, it was found that two of the party were missing and that they had secured about fifty head of Pawnee horses and had taken four scalps, young Red Cloud being the proud possessor of one of these. After resting a few hours the party then took up its homeward march, traveling all that night.[4]

The next day they traveled until the middle of the afternoon when they decided that they were securely distant from the Pawnees, and feeling fatigued they went into camp and remained there until the following morning,

when they again took up their journey, traveling by easy
stages, and reaching home on the evening of the seventh
day after the fight, having been absent sixteen days.

As the party neared the village, friends and relatives
came out to meet them on horseback, and all the knolls
and rising ground about the village were covered with
women and children shouting a joyous welcome to the
returning warriors, mingled with the weird, pathetic cries
and groans of the relatives of the two men who were killed
by the Pawnees, news of which loss they had already received by horsemen who were continually galloping to and
fro between the advancing party and the village. Each one
seemed to vie with the other in contributing his or her
share to the general excitement incident to the return of
a large party.[5]

When the warriors entered the village, each one was
surrounded by his kinswomen, who, after various mani-
festations of welcome, would take the rein of the bridle
and lead the horse to the lodge where the brave would
dismount and enter. One would think that here he would
wish to remain and rest, but however this may be, he is
not permitted to do so, for scarcely has he put away his
trappings of war and settled himself to rest in his own
lodge among his family, when there is a call at the tent
door. This is generally made by some little girl, who, after
opening the flap of the lodge inserts her head and shoulders and says "Uncle" or "Cousin, Mother calls you," and
then she scampers home, soon to be sent to some other
lodge on a similar errand.

The person thus called arises and wrapping his blanket around him, goes to the lodge named, where he is

regaled with the best Indian repast obtainable. While he feasts, he undergoes a series of interrogations recounting all the incidents of his journey and fight, and scarcely does he finish his story and meal before he is called to another lodge, where he goes through the same performance.

Thus the feast is kept up throughout the village until nearly daylight, the returned braves and other notables being the special guests. But simultaneously with this feasting and visiting, there is another feast in progress in the village—the feast of sorrow, and from the darkened lodges in which the fires have been permitted to smolder, and from the tops and sides of the hills that surround the camp there come the weird wails and harrowing cries of the families of the warriors who came not back. But the intensity of these people's expressions of grief necessarily shortens its duration at any one time, so that calm soon succeeds their outbursts of sorrow, yet it continues to recur during a year or more.

The next day was spent in preparing for the festivities that follow the successful termination of a tilt with the enemy. A great medicine pole was erected in an open space, around which huge piles of wood are placed at a proper distance; great kettles of food were prepared for the occasion, and as darkness approached the wood was lighted and the sound of drums gave notice that the dance had begun. This dance lasted for two days and nights without cessation; as fast as the participants became exhausted they retired for recuperation and their places were immediately filled by those in waiting.

It is the custom among the Sioux to permit only those who have killed or struck an enemy, and such of their near relations as wish, to paint themselves a hideous black upon these occasions, that being a mark of great distinction. The black paint is also sometimes used by individuals to indicate that they contemplate some daring deed; but in the war dance this practice is confined to those who have gained some signal victory over an enemy, and as a consequence of this custom, many grim visages were seen by the glare of the fire, going through their grotesque pantomime, in imitation of their respective encounters with some foe, holding the scalps they had taken aloft on sticks, and talking with great bravado of the wonderful feats performed in securing these, to them, treasures of war.

Each warrior who participates in these festivities can prove his pretensions to consideration for bravery by displaying his scalps or wounds, but he can also prove them in another manner very acceptable—in fact this very material proof cannot be dispensed with for any length of time without seriously affecting the brave's reputation. He must have horses, stolen or captured, which he must give away to the old, the poor, the weak, the sick, and the cowards, any of which circumstances may be mentioned by the warrior with impunity upon presentation.

Ambush

RED CLOUD SOON FOLLOWED his initial success against the Pawnee tribe with an even greater feat of bravery against the Crows, another of the Oglalas' implacable enemies.[1] The ambush of the Crow raiding party, recounted here, occurred in present Wyoming near the trading post of Fort Laramie. Built of logs in 1834 by fur traders, the first post—and its adobe successor—drew Plains tribes interested in commerce and became an economic hub for the Western Sioux. The young Red Cloud could not have avoided becoming a longtime observer of the white man's ways.[2]

Historical records from the fort's initial years, though, are sparse, and its general histories make no mention of this Red Cloud story. Then again, white chroniclers on the Plains rarely recorded the countless intertribal contests unless whites were present as eyewitnesses or the clashes disrupted trade.

After the gala days of feasting and dancing were over, and the village had resumed its usual appearance, a council was held among the old men of the tribe at which it was decided to remain where they were during the winter, and, as it was getting late in the fall, hunting parties were sent out to secure their winter supply of buffalo meat. These parties found plenty of buffalo on Hat Creek, about fifty miles northeast of the village at Fort Laramie, and they soon killed and cured a large quantity of meat besides securing a great number of robes, returning to the main village just as the severe storms of winter began.

It was in the month of March following, when the snow was very deep, and unusually severe storms were still raging at short intervals, that the news was brought to camp that a war party of fourteen Crows had been sighted about twenty-five miles up the Platte River near the mouth of what is now known as Bitter Cottonwood Creek; as was customary with the Crows, they were all on foot.[3] Their object in approaching so large a body of Sioux could only be that of stealing horses under the cover of the storms and getting away unobserved, but they had been discovered by a Sioux who had been out deer hunting, and without knowing that they had been seen, they were doomed.

Early the next morning a large body of Sioux started out to intercept them. After crossing the Platte River, the Sioux kept south for a short distance, entering the low hills that lie between the Platte and the Laramie rivers, then turning to the west they followed the general course of the Platte, covered by the low hills and a severe storm. After traveling about eight miles, they again changed their course to the north to conform to the winding of the river, and in going over the brow of a long hill, they saw the Crows just entering the valley at its base near what is known as Warm Springs.

The Sioux immediately sounded their war cry and charged. The Crows, astounded at their discovery and the number of their assailants, and weak and worn from fatigue and exposure, contemplated the approaching Sioux for a few seconds, and then seeming to realize the hopelessness of their position drew their blankets over their heads and dropped down in the snow, face downward, on which the Sioux advanced and killed them where they lay. Red Cloud was one of the foremost riders, and he struck three of the prostrated Crows with his bow, but killed none of them, for the reason that among the Indians, more bravery is considered to be displayed by striking a living enemy than by killing him. In so doing they take chances of being shot themselves. No sooner had Red Cloud hit the three Crows than they were killed by the general firing of the party.

The Sioux well understood that no glory had been achieved by the killing of the Crows in this manner, and the event was celebrated at the village only because of the death of the fourteen enemies and not on account of any display of valor on the part of the participants, excepting Red Cloud, who had struck the Crows while they were still alive and armed.

3

War with the Omahas

WARFARE BETWEEN TRIBES often originated with one tribe infringing on the hunting grounds of another. The Omaha tribe, whose earthlodge villages in eastern Nebraska flanked the Missouri River, cautiously ventured to the western buffalo range for seasonal hunts. The Lakotas jealously guarded these lands as their own, and confrontations between the two tribes were inevitable.[1]

Unlike the hopelessly outnumbered Crow raiders in the previous story, here was an enemy force that matched the Oglala camp. The somewhat protracted fight, a rarity by Plains Indian standards, indicates two tipi villages of relatively equal strength, each unable to inflict a crushing blow on the other, neither suffering devastating casualties. Nevertheless, within this conservative arena of feint and parry, Red Cloud performed another brave feat in helping rescue a wounded comrade.

Drifting about their vast possessions in that happy, careless manner peculiar to the western tribes of those days, we find the Oglala village five years later encamped on the northern branch of what is known as Prairie Creek in Hall County. The Sioux were traveling and their course lay down the creek, its confluence with the North Platte [actually the Platte River, not the North Platte] being the objective point, when within one day's journey of this place, their scouts reported the sight of smoke near the mouth of the creek. The Sioux immediately came to a halt and encamped in a safe place. A sufficient number of fighting men were left to protect the village, while a large body went forward to investigate the cause of the smoke. Approaching the place cautiously they discovered a large village of Omahas, who were engaged in some of their tribal festivities. A great dance was in progress, in the center of which a small pole from which floated an Indian flag was standing; the Sioux quickly decided upon a surprise, the charge to be made through that portion of the village farthest removed from the congregated dancers. Red Cloud conceived the idea that this would call immediately the warriors from the dance, decided to capture the flag, and soon formed a little party of his own for this purpose.

The charge was begun. For a moment panic seized the Omahas, but they soon rallied to meet their foes. Red Cloud and his little company of five closed together and added to the general consternation by setting fire to the first lodge they came to; then backing away from the main party, they made a dash for the flag, but the Omahas, divining their intentions, quickly sent a shower of arrows whizzing among them. They dashed on, however, through the flying arrows and scathing bullets. Red Cloud had just raised his tomahawk to hew down the sapling that supported the flag, when a warrior by his side was hit with a rifle ball and would have fallen from his horse, but that Red Cloud, dropping his tomahawk, caught him by the arm, another companion catching him by the other arm. At the same time they turned their horses and thus holding him in the saddle, the little party galloped back to the main body, which by this time had drawn off towards the bluff near the western edge of the village.

The Sioux whom Red Cloud had taken from the field began to revive, and it was found he was only wounded, so together with three others who were also wounded, he was taken to the village where all of them recovered in the course of time.

The Omahas in the meantime had gathered in force between their village and the attacking Sioux, and, as most of them had their horses brought to them and were mounted, they were now masters of the situation so far as the safety of their village was concerned. The Sioux then began to maneuver for a feigned attack upon the south side of the village; then suddenly changing their course made a charge toward the north side with all the rapidity that the speed of their horses could accomplish. But the Omahas were alert for such a move, for at that time and many years thereafter, Indians did their principal fighting with bows and arrows, clubs and tomahawks, a few possessing old muskets and rifles. Therefore, stratagem and rapidity and rapidly executed movements constituted their most important tactics. Thus like met like. The Omahas quickly flanked the charging Sioux and drove them from their course over the bridge to the north of the village.

The Sioux then returned to their village, and that evening a council was held at which it was decided to move camp nearer to the Omahas, so that they could have a larger fighting force in the field and still be near enough to their field [camp?] in case the Omahas should attempt to attack them. Accordingly, during the night the Sioux village was moved to within a few miles of the Omaha camp, and the next morning hostilities were resumed and continued in a desultory manner for two days, during which time no one was killed but many were "comfortably" wounded—that is, just enough to assist them in their Indian record making. The real danger in those ancient Indian fights when the opposing forces were equally divided, was about on a par with the games of modern football or cricket; they were enchantingly picturesque, but not deadly.

On the afternoon of the last day of this fight, there was a cessation of movements and a parley held between the opposing forces at a distance through the medium of the sign language, each side making plain to the other that they were considered intruders and the right of possession to the hunting grounds of that section was the question in dispute and the object for which they had been fighting.[2]

The Sioux, as a point of stratagem, endeavored to inveigle the Omahas into a closer council where the matter could be talked over and agreed upon, but all such advances were met by the Omahas by the waving of a blanket, which in the sign language signified, "Come and fight us," but the Sioux, deciding that they had had recreation enough, declined these proffered courtesies and repairing to their village, were soon again on the move toward the great interior of their estate, that country lying in and about the Laramie Valley and the Black Hills.

4

Raid on the Crows

RED CLOUD HAD CLEARLY BEGUN to make a name for himself when he joined a horse-stealing expedition against the Crow tribe, whose ever-diminishing homeland included southeastern Montana and northeastern Wyoming. A frequent target of raiders throughout the early nineteenth century, the Crows suffered greatly at the hands of the expanding Lakota nation. The struggle between the two tribes continued largely unabated for three decades following this incident.[1]

Red Cloud's decision to proceed to the Crow village in advance of his colleagues resulted in the theft of three hundred horses, an impressive but manageable feat for a party of thirty braves. For instance, in another Native American narrative, tribal historian Joseph Medicine Crow told of two Crow men who once returned the favor and came away from a Lakota camp with fifteen Sioux horses apiece, a splendid achievement.[2]

Red Cloud's success on this raid continued to enhance his growing reputation as a leader.

Red Cloud next joined a large war party organized to go against the Crows, who were thought to be encamped on the Yellowstone River, near the mouth of Rosebud Creek, in what is now Custer County, Montana, a distance about one hundred fifty miles from this Sioux village. The party, leaving their camp in the morning, crossed the Tongue River on the afternoon of the fifth day and camped for that night about ten miles from the river on a small stream.

There is a great contrast between the conduct of Indians in and about camp on a war party and that of a regular village. When a party is out and approaching the enemy's country, everything is conducted in the quietest manner possible; traveling is done through the lowest valleys and the deepest gorges, and along the edges of small timbered creeks, while scouts are continually creeping about the highest points on either side of the main body. Many times travel is done by night, and during the day the war party is hidden; their horses are kept from grazing about and are held in some secluded place, easy of access by their owners.

At this camp on this particular night everything was conducted in the usual precautionary manner, but there was great difference of opinion among the members of the party in regard to their proximity to the Crow village. Red Cloud was among the few who believed that the Crows were quite near; accordingly after a repast of dried meat and water had been partaken of, he selected a young Minneconjou in whom he had confidence, and preparing themselves quietly with strong moccasins and a lariat rope, they waited until the others retired for the night; then stealing away on foot they ascended a high ridge about two miles west of the camp where they took a look for camp fires, or some reflection of light that would indicate camp fires in the direction where the Crows were supposed to be living.

It was a still night and dark, but nothing could be seen that would tend to locate the Crow village. While resting here and talking over the situation, they thought they could detect a faint sound borne to them occasionally from the direction of the Yellowstone River. For a long time they listened intently but could catch nothing distinctly, but they concluded to advance in the direction from which the sound came. After journeying about ten miles they ascended to the summit of another hill and halted for a rest and to take observations. Here they were rewarded by being able to distinguish the sound of a drum. Continuing their course more cautiously yet steadily, the sound grew more and more distinct as they advanced until it began to get late in the night, when the sound ceased altogether.

While thus engaged in a whispered conversation over the situation, they became aware of something moving in the valley below them. They secreted themselves among the pines and watched and listened. Presently the gray dawn of light made objects distinguishable, and they saw that about fifty head of horses were quietly feeding on the small grassy plateau that lay between them and the next pine hills to the northwest. Moving cautiously through the herd they caught each a fine horse, and mounting them, proceeded to quietly round up the herd, keeping a good lookout all the while for some approaching herder.

Just as they were moving away with the horses, Red Cloud saw a Crow Indian sitting against a pine tree about a hundred yards distant.[3] He had his back to the herd, which had evidently grazed away from him. His blanket was drawn over his head, which was resting upon his hands. His elbows were supported by resting upon his knees. Readily surmising that he was asleep, Red Cloud told his companion to keep the horses moving slowly around the base of the hills, and he would go and kill him.

Riding slowly until within a few paces of his unsuspecting victim he suddenly made a charge. Wielding his war club with terrific force, he brought it down, aiming it at the herder's head, but, as the Crow moved suddenly a little, he missed his aim and struck the tree. Instantly the sleeper sprang to his feet and throwing his blanket backward gave a terrific yell and started to run. Red Cloud, who had deftly slipped the noose on the handle of his war club over the horn of his saddle, now took his bow from his left hand, and drawing the feathered end of an arrow through his mouth, quickly placed it in his bow and sent it whirring into the body of the receding Crow, who staggered and fell; as he did so, Red Cloud jumped from his horse and taking his victim's knife from his belt, stabbed him with it until he was dead. He then took the scalp lock and mounting his horse joined his companion, who was hurrying the herd toward the Sioux camp. When

Red Cloud came up, the speed of the herd was increased to its utmost capacity.

About noon that day they saw the large party of Sioux coming, and Red Cloud said to his friend, "Now we will be whipped or scolded, for we have not only broken rules by going out without the direction of the chiefs, but we have stolen so many horses that they will be jealous." Thus the two were mentally preparing themselves for their reprimand, when they saw their friends consult together and then come charging with all their fury right through the herd they were driving, scattering them in all directions.

They approached Red Cloud and his companion with their whips raised and were just about to perform the usual act of "soldiering a delinquent" when the two head chiefs of the party, Old Man Afraid of His Horse and Brave Bear, who had been consulting together apart from the others, hallooed to them to stop. As the Indians obeyed this command, the two chiefs rode up to the two delinquents, and Brave Bear said, "My sons, you have stolen a great number of horses, and there must be a large village of women and children where you got them." Red Cloud told them that they had seen no village nor women and children, but told them what he had done, displaying the scalp he had taken from the Crow. Then he was loudly applauded, and a general desire seized the party to go on believing that the operations of the two young men had been performed in such a secluded spot and at such a remote distance from the village, that the chances of its being discovered immediately were very small.

Accordingly it was decided that Red Cloud and his companion should go on with their horses to the camp they had left the evening before and remain there while the main party proceeded, winding through the hills in such a manner as to secure them the greatest security against detection. When night came, they were still some distance from the Crow village, but approaching nearer and nearer, alternately halting and moving, they gained the point of vantage they desired long before daybreak. The rest of the night was spent in arranging for the morning attack.

At daylight, when the party of thirty Sioux dashed up in full view of the Crows, there was a great furor of excitement in the village. Many herders who were just starting out after the herds turned back and prepared to engage in the coming battle.

For two hours the Sioux charged and countercharged and rode in a circle around the village, but as they had no intention of engaging in actual fighting if it could be avoided, they always kept at a safe distance. Finally the watch that had been left on the top of one of the highest hills gave the smoke signal which was agreed upon, and they knew that the small parties detached for the purpose while the attack was made were well on their way with the Crows' horses; then they began to fall back, fighting as they were sometimes compelled to do, by those pursuing Crows who had succeeded in getting their mounts, but as the number of such were few, the Sioux had no difficulty in making a covered retreat for their companions.

They all reached their rendezvous by sundown that evening, and after changing horses started for their village on the Belle Fourche, traveling all that night in order to put as great a distance between them and the Crows as soon as possible. It was found after they had counted the horses that they had captured nearly three hundred head and had not lost a man; therefore, their return to the village on the eleventh day from their departure was one of unsullied triumph.[4]

Shoshones

By 1849 RED CLOUD'S PEERS had accorded the young warrior the recognition he sought. His military accomplishments may be considered even more impressive and significant if he did, in fact, implement new tactics, referred to in this story as a new "system of small war parties." Once again the Red Cloud narrative, narrowly focused as it is on one man's experiences, may shed light on the broader strategies of Lakota expansionism.

It is clear, however, that the nature of Plains Indian warfare changed after the appearance and prevalence of efficient firearms. Exchanging bullets was far more dangerous than exchanging arrows. The earlier tilt against the Omaha village might have produced many more casualties had it occurred a generation later.[1]

Mention of a "Hawkins" rifle may surprise some readers. Charles E. Hanson, Jr., in his insightful book on the subject, *The Hawken Rifle: Its Place in History*, effectively discounts the notion that this muzzleloader was the mountain man's firearm of choice. At the end of the mountain man period (about 1840), however, Fort Laramie traders sold to their Plains Indian customers several of the Plains rifles made by the Hawken brothers of St. Louis.[2]

Setting aside matters of armament, yet another neighbor, the Shoshone or Snake tribe, received the brunt of Red Cloud's attention in 1849. The eastern Shoshones ranged across present southern Idaho, northeast Utah, and western Wyoming, where trapper-trader caravans and emigrant trains on their way west enountered them.[3] That Red Cloud made no mention in this story or others of the great rush of whites westward, the congestion around Fort Laramie, and the cholera epidemics of 1849–1854 is typical for his narrative.[4] His concerns lay with his people's traditional enemies or his personal rivals, not with whites, against whom no real glory could be gained.

During the next few years the Indians in general had made some advancement in their mode of warfare; at least it had become a more dangerous pastime. Immigration had begun to pass through their country, and they were more frequently visited by traders, and as one of the consequences the Hawkins rifle became a weapon in general use. Red Cloud, who had so rapidly risen in the estimation of his people as a brave young man, had become one of the head warriors of his tribe; he had introduced the system of small war parties composed of from eight to twelve men over whom he was always accorded the command by unanimous consent. In fact, his bravery and sagacity had become so generally acknowledged that his name was synonymous with success. Strongly supported by a large body of admiring adherents, yet secretly opposed by the envy and jealousy of rivals, his fame continued to increase and spread until the stories of his numerous exploits were told about the camp fires of all the different bands that had constituted the Sioux nation.

It is thus we find Red Cloud in the spring of 1849, still in the flush and vigor of youth, being twenty-eight years of age.

The Oglalas were camped on the west side of the Black Hills on the head of Powder River near the base of Pumpkin Butte, when Red Cloud, again growing weary of the monotony of camp life, quietly organized a party of twelve warriors for the purpose of making a foray against the Snake, or Shoshone, Indians.

Taking a southwesterly course, they had traveled about one hundred miles when a discussion arose among the members of the party as to the propriety of going forward or returning to the village. Red Cloud, who had no intention of retracing his steps until he had accomplished his object, began to investigate the cause of the disaffection. He soon found that the chief cause was Black Eagle, a man who had long been one of his trustiest warriors, but who, having grown jealous of his leader's popularity, sought to embarrass this undertaking by creating mutiny. This he endeavored to do by telling his comrades that they were all lost among the mountains, that Red Cloud did not know where they were going, and that they were foolish to be dragged along day after day in a place where their enemies could so easily ambush them. This, coming from an indisputably brave man, had its effect, and, had Red Cloud not discovered it in time, it might have resulted in sending him back to the village under a cloud; but having discovered the situation, he acted at once.

Finding that Black Eagle had succeeded in gaining an evil influence over but three of his party, Red Cloud, after consulting with the rest of the men, who agreed to stand by him, prepared to start from the halting place as if nothing had occurred, paying no attention to the sullen mutterings of Black Eagle and his friends. He proposed to retrace his steps a short distance and ascend a high mountain that stood in the rear and get their bearings. The mutineers readily assented to this proposal, believing it was a turn of affairs in their favor. When they had reached the summit of the mountain, as had been previously arranged, the rest of the party circled about the four disaffected Indians, and Red Cloud, addressing Black Eagle, and pointing to the east said, "Do you see that high blue ridge away yonder? At the foot of that mountain is our village; there is where the women are. Go! You cannot get lost. You can go back over the same trail you came. There is lots of game; get some of your party to kill it for you, and, when there is another war party to go out, you had better stay at home and send your women."

Having said this with the air and gesture of one who meant what he said, and was prepared to enforce his commands, Red Cloud turned and followed by his faithful seven filed down the mountain on the same side as they ascended, leaving Black Eagle and the other three standing alone on the summit.

The Sioux are Indians of the plains, and they were never fully contented while in a mountainous country. They once owned the Black Hills, and their favorite resort either in summer or winter was around the base of this cluster of mountains on either side, but rarely if ever did they penetrate the interior of these hills to remain any length of time.

Nevertheless they now steadily pursued their way during the remainder of that day and camped that night in a gorge of the mountain from which place they could distinguish noises that their experience told them must come from an Indian village of considerable size.

About midnight they started in the direction they believed the village to be, and by daylight they were among the hills overlooking the Big Horn Valley. Placing their horses in a safe place where the walls of the canyon formed a natural corral for the main part, and leaving one of their number to watch them, the others started on foot to reconnoitre. Ascending a pine mountain nearby they were gratified to see a beautiful valley spread out before them through which wound the Big Horn River, on the east bank of which was located a large Shoshone village a short distance above where the Wind River joins it on the west.

After studying the situation for awhile Red Cloud decided to rest and watch during the day, and accordingly one man was left on the mountain and one over the horses as watchers, being relieved at intervals. This gave the whole party an opportunity to get some much needed rest. Red Cloud remained in the mountain with the watch and looked long and intently at the great cluster of white lodges with the smoke curling from their tops, the Indians hurrying to and fro, some after wood, others off to the hills after their horses, while others were driving their herds into the Big Horn to drink. Then he gave his instructions to the watch and rolled himself in his blanket and slept. About two o'clock in the afternoon he arose and went down to where the rest were and after refreshing themselves with food and water, they got everything in readiness. Leading their horses to the foot of the mountain on which their watch was stationed, they secreted themselves among the pines and joined the watch. The village now presented a different appearance than during the morning. It was now the gala part of the day and in one place could be seen a number of Indians horse racing; in another a large congregation were partaking of a feast; in still another a great number of young men and women were engaged in the exciting game of shinny ball,[5] and hunters were continually filing into camp with their ponies loaded down with game.

As the hidden Sioux waited and watched, the sun began to glide over the mountain peaks to the west, and, as the shades of evening approached, Red Cloud remarked this fact, and after a little while they saw in the village the operations for which they had been waiting. The Shoshones began to drive their horses in all directions to the hills for the night, and, as the herds left the village, the Sioux discussed their number, the direction and distance they were being driven, and the number of men driving them, which was never greater than three and usually one or two.

While Red Cloud and his party were thus engaged in observation and comment, they saw a herd of about sixty head of horses coming on a spry trot in their direction, driven by two Shoshones. Quietly withdrawing to the base of the mountain they secured their horses and continued to watch their approaching prey. As the herd passed around the base of a low projecting hill out of sight of the village, the Sioux filed through a small pass in the mountain and came upon them from the rear with such suddenness that the Shoshones were appalled.

The excited herd stampeded in the direction that the Sioux wished to go, while the herders realizing their position, fired upon the advancing Sioux, hitting one of their horses and dismounting the rider; but they had no time to reload, for the Sioux, desiring to avoid firing off their guns for fear of attracting the attention of the Indians at the village, rushed upon the two herders with war clubs and tomahawks, and it was here that Red Cloud had the opportunity of gratifying the crowning ambition of an Indian warrior's life, that is first to strike, then to kill, and then to scalp his adversary. The other Shoshone was killed and scalped by others of the party, and the Sioux who had been dismounted during the fray now mounted one of the Shoshone horses, and the party started after the stampeded herd, which they soon had under control. They took them through the mountains, over the same trail they traveled the previous day. They kept on all day and night, and by noon the next day it became necessary to stop for rest.

Having slept the afternoon they were agreeably surprised just before dark by the arrival of Red Cloud's
brother and brother-in-law, Big Spider and Little Bad
Wolf, who brought news that the big Sioux village had
moved to Fort Laramie.[6] They said it had been the intention to wait until Red Cloud's party returned, but upon
the arrival of Black Eagle who brought news that the
party was scattered and lost in the Big Horn Mountains
and that they were probably all killed by the Shoshones,
the village, with the exception of a few lodges that were
left as a guide and to search for the missing, had concluded to move on to the fort.

After the watch had been put on duty, a small fire
was started in a place that would preclude the light from
being seen at a distance. The fore part of the night was
spent in roasting deer meat and exchanging news, Big
Spider and Little Bad Wolf giving all the happenings in
the village, including Black Eagle's stories and conduct,
in exchange for the thrilling adventure of Red Cloud and
his party.

Next morning Red Cloud decided to take a southeasterly course to Fort Laramie, and Big Spider and Little
Bad Wolf went back to their old camp to move and overtake the village. Moving on leisurely through a country
full of game the Sioux and their herd of stolen horses
had an opportunity to recuperate after their long forced
march from the Big Horn River, and when within two
days travel from their destination they stopped on a small
stream now called LaBonte that runs into the Platte from
the south. Here they killed a number of elk and packed
several of their horses with meat; then they started for

the village. Having crossed the little stream about fifteen miles southeast of LaBonte, now known as Horseshoe Creek, they were moving through a narrow defile in the mountain, when an incident occurred that first alarmed and then amused them. Suddenly their horses became excited, running in every direction, their pack horses were rearing and snorting, and the rattling and clashing of their packs added greatly to the confusion. At first the Sioux thought they were entrapped in an ambuscade, but they soon got sight of one of their horses that was heavily packed with fresh meat, on top of which was perched with majestic mein a huge mountain lion, an animal that partakes of the peculiarities of both the wild cat and the panther. It had evidently sprung from a projecting rock, attracted by the odor of the fresh meat, but, as soon as it saw the Indians and the general consternation it had caused, it rolled to the ground and was soon lost among the stunted pines.

The day following this incident the party had the satisfaction of entering the home village with their game and horses, amid the plaudits of an admiring throng. The success of this trip after the desertion of Black Eagle and his companions greatly added to the renown of Red Cloud as a warrior, hunter, and leader of men, for he had not only brought back to his friends the trophies of war that invariably incited them to the performance of their highest festival rites, but he had also brought back the necessary provisions to furnish the foundation of all their gala revelries, the feast.

Shooting Bull Bear

NATIVE AMERICAN AUTOBIOGRAPHIES, if they remain faithful to their principals' order of presentation, do not depend on a strict chronology in their narration, a characteristic manifested with this story. The account of Bull Bear's shooting not only falls out of the chronological order of the preceding stories, the assigned year is also clearly incorrect.

Four reliable sources place the event earlier than 1845, the year assigned by Red Cloud, Charles Allen, and/or Sam Deon. Francis Parkman, Jr., the eminent American historian and author of the classic *Oregon Trail* (which first appeared in book form in 1849 under a different title), heard the story in 1846 and wrote that it had occurred "five or six years earlier." Rufus B. Sage, an educated fur trapper and author of the invaluable narrative *Rocky Mountain Life* (1846), traveled through the area and dated the event to late 1841. Finally and most convincingly, American Horse and Iron Crow, nineteenth-century Oglala tribal historians who recorded the major events in their people's history, separately placed Bull Bear's demise during the same winter of 1841–1842.[1]

Nevertheless, this documentation relating to a Red Cloud story helps bolster his reputation as a chronicler. Unlike Parkman and Sage, who recorded secondhand sketches, Red Cloud, an important participant, presents an eyewitness account. Considerable weight should also be given to Red Cloud's version of the origin tale of the Kiyuksa ("Ki-ya-ksa"), or Cut-off band of Oglalas.[2]

The Oglalas remained in the neighborhood of Fort Laramie, moving from one locality to another, until the year 1845. In the early spring of that year, Red Cloud with a party of ten made a foray into the Ute country. They crossed Crow Creek, near where the city of Cheyenne now stands, and working south, entered the mountains near the head waters of the Cache LaPoudre River in Colorado. In those days the Ute Indians roamed all over that country and were continually at war with the plains Indians—the Sioux especially.[3]

Red Cloud and his party had not entered the mountains a very great distance when they became aware of the presence of the Utes by the horse tracks which they discovered leading down a small stream. Following up this trail they soon came in sight of two small temporary lodges on the banks of the creek about which were hanging great quantities of meat drying in the sun. They sought to make their approach stealthily, but while yet within some distance of the lodges they saw one man and two women hurriedly leave them on horseback, and they knew by this that they had been discovered.

On arriving at the lodges they found them deserted, and they also found pots filled with meat cooking on the fire and other evidences of hurried flight. After eating their dinner they loaded their horses with all the dried meat they cared to take, together with other trophies secured among the effects of the absent Utes and began to retrace their steps.

As they were traveling leisurely along and were winding around the side of a mountain among the pine trees, they suddenly came to a halt, for they heard someone singing. The song grew more distinct, and, on looking across the gulch to the side of the opposite mountain, they discovered the singer—a Ute as they supposed—who was coming down through the rocks and timber with his pony heavily laden with deer. As he was coming directly toward them, all unconscious of the fate that awaited him, the Sioux decided to wait until he had crossed over the gully between the mountains. During this time, which was not long, they held a whispered conversation, coming to the conclusion that this lone hunter was the husband of one of the women who had so precipitately left the lodge an hour or two before.

With the eager expectancy of tigers awaiting prey, these savages watched the approach of their victim through the swaying boughs of the low pines until he had reached the fatal spot. Then there was the sharp ring of a Hawkins rifle, and the Ute lay dead and bleeding upon the ground, while a few paces away the pony with his burden of fresh meat stood leisurely nipping the short grass as though nothing had happened.

Pony, scalp, and trappings were taken by the Sioux, and their homeward march continued. Striking what is now the Black Hills of Wyoming where the tributaries of Chugwater come winding around the base of Iron Mountain, they followed this creek down to what has since been known as Point of Rocks. Here they came to the village of the Koya (meaning "and two also"), one of the subdivisions of the Oglalas, and from them they learned that the Oglala village had divided into bands that were camped at different places along the creek for convenience and that only a short distance below the Koya village the Bad Face camp was located. As this was the family band to which Red Cloud and most of his party belonged, they pushed their way on toward their own village.

Red Cloud had not been home long until he saw and heard enough to convince him that considerable animosity had sprung up between his band and the Koyas. Little private bickerings had been multiplied and magnified until they sometimes wore a serious aspect, but these usually passed off as family troubles are wont to do. The Koyas were in the habit of displaying their insolence to the other bands, for the reason that they were numerically stronger than any of the others, the Bad Face being the only band that came near being equal in strength. And again their self-importance was somewhat intensified by the fact that the most prominent chief of the Oglalas at that time was Bull Bear and he belonged to the Koya band.[4] Yet the Bad Faces had never been subjected to annoyances from any of their neighbors on account of numbering among their warriors such men as Red Cloud and his numerous and powerful relationship. But one misunderstanding followed another until the climax was reached.

A young Bad Face, who was very much disliked by Chief Bull Bear and others of the Koyas, stole a Koya woman, a perfectly legitimate way of obtaining a wife according to one of the Indian customs, provided all the parties interested are friends; otherwise it is looked upon as an insult to the bride's relatives. Upon this occasion the "old folks" were seriously opposed to the young man in question, and, as the girl was related to Chief Bull Bear, it was decided to have her back and chastise the young Lochinvar.

One serious obstacle that presented itself to Chief Bull Bear's mind was the fact of the presence in the Bad village of an old Indian by the name of Trunk or Box. He was known to be one of the bravest of the brave among all the Indians. He was no chief, but his stubborn fighting qualities caused most of the Indians to fear him. He was an uncle of Red Cloud, but Chief Bull Bear did not take the latter into consideration. Trunk was the man he wished to be absent from the village when they should go down to execute their bluff, and, as he was managing the affair, he concluded to wait until such an opportunity presented itself.

But as time passed, some of his people who had been out to the south towards the Platte River came in bringing some whiskey that they had obtained from some traders or travelers. This hastened a climax in which Chief Bull Bear met his fate.

As they had plenty of liquor and were more or less under the influence of it, they conceived the idea of inviting Trunk over to have a time with them. When he should be sufficiently drunk, they would proceed to execute their plans without his interference.

Trunk accepted the invitation but failed to get very drunk; at any rate when Chief Bull Bear and his party started for the Bad Face village, Trunk was there almost as soon as they were. When the Koyas reached the Bad Face village, they met several Indians, one of whom happened to be the father of the young man who had stolen the Koya girl. Being under the influence of liquor they shot him.

About this time the voice of Trunk was heard hallooing as he approached the place, "Are you going to lay there and be killed? Where are all the young men? Where is Red Cloud? Red Cloud, are you going to disgrace your father's name?"

This harangue and the unexpected shot had raised the Bad Faces, and many of the young men rushed out to meet the insolent intruders, Red Cloud among them.

They opened fire on the Koyas at once, and one of the shots struck Chief Bull Bear in the leg and brought him to the ground in a sitting position. Red Cloud rushing toward him shot him through the head, exclaiming as he did so, "You are the cause of this."

Following up their advantage the Bad Faces dashed on to the Koya village, but excitement and terror had preceded them, and they found it nearly deserted. Their ardor having cooled a little by this time, they contented themselves with gathering up a lot of women, children, and ponies and taking them back to their camp.

The death of Bull Bear and the capture of the women, children, and ponies terminated the difficulty with the Koyas, who after treating with their conquerors for the return of their families moved over to the South Platte River where they held a council for the purpose of electing a new chief. At this council the name of the little band was also changed. Several names were proposed, and there was much discussion, but at last an old man, seeing a little garter snake wriggling through the grass, caught it up and holding it by the head and tail bit it in two in the middle, exclaiming, "This shall be our name, 'Ki-ya-ksa,'" meaning literally "bitten in two." The general translation, however, is incorrectly "cut off" by which name the band has ever since been known. The son of Bull Bear was elected to his father's place and assumed his name.

On the death of Bull Bear, the younger, the band remained without a chief until after the Sioux treaty of 1868. Red Cloud was then recognized chief of the Sioux and was empowered by the United States commission to select sub-chiefs. At the suggestion of his friend, Nicholas Janis, then one of the interpreters, Red Cloud appointed Little Wound, nephew of the first Bull Bear, to the sub-chieftaincy and by this stroke of policy extinguished the last smoldering embers of resentment in the Cut-Off band.[5]

7

Raid on the Pawnees

RED CLOUD'S SUCCESSION of triumphs ended with this raid on a Pawnee village in Nebraska, in which he suffered a severe wound. The story is corroborated in part by rancher James H. Cook, who heard the incident from Red Cloud himself.[1] If not for the actions of his comrades, Red Cloud's career would have ended abruptly.

No date is assigned to this story, and it is unclear how much time had elapsed since the Shoshone raid. By the late 1840s, however, the Pawnee tribe had abandoned its village sites in the Middle Loup drainage in central Nebraska, which calls into question both the time and the place the narrative states for this event. Seeking respite from the annual attacks by the Sioux, the Pawnees sought the relative safety of a more defensible, eastern locale.[2]

Red Cloud's next expedition was with a war party of twenty against the Pawnees who were then camped on the Middle Loup. On the eighth day after leaving their village, they came to the Pawnee country and secreting themselves sent out scouts to ascertain the whereabouts of the village and the strength of their enemies. This required several days. The scouts who made their advance toward the place where the village was supposed to be had to exercise the utmost caution and slip from hill to hill whenever they got an opportunity, for it was no uncommon thing to see from their hiding places some lone horseman galloping over the prairie. Several times their advance was checked by such an occurrence as this, but by watching the general course of the riders they were enabled to fix the location of the village with a considerable degree of accuracy, and with such information they would return to their party when night came for provisions, instructions, and a new start. In this manner two or three days passed before the scouts got information that would enable them to determine what to do. They learned that the Pawnees were camped in a straggling, disconnected sort of way for several miles along the Loup below them and that they were cultivating patches of Indian corn. They therefore decided to make their attack on the first cluster of families that they came to in traveling down the river from their hiding place.

Accordingly about three o'clock in the morning they took up their march in this direction and neared the village a little before daylight. They waited under cover of the small trees that skirted the banks of the stream until morning, and at daylight they saw a Pawnee man and woman coming toward a small field of corn that lay out a little way from the river. They waited until they [the man and the woman] had reached their destination and had begun to pull weeds from among the corn. Then they swooped down upon them and shot the man to death with arrows and scalped him, but the woman was left unmolested. Whirling from the field where they committed this barbarous deed, they charged the lodges a little farther on, shouting and yelling as was their custom. The Pawnees were not wholly surprised, having seen the Sioux in time to make a show of resistance, and, while the women and children were running to the brush, the men were firing at the advancing party.

The Sioux rode right into their village and the fighting was desperate for a few minutes; two Pawnees were brained by the well-mounted Sioux, and one of the Sioux was killed by a shot from a musket, though the fighting was done almost entirely with bows, arrows, and tomahawks. One Pawnee woman, who had left the house and was running for the brush after the fight had begun, was ridden down by a Sioux who caught her by the hair and stopped her. Then he made signs telling her to mount behind him and make no resistance, or he would kill her. She complied with his first demand, and the Sioux wheeled his horse and began riding away from the rear of his party. He had gone but a short distance, however, when the Pawnee woman slipped her knife from its scabbard under her belt and reaching around in front of her captor by one quick movement literally cut him in two. As he rolled to the ground, she snatched the reins and turning the horse around started at full speed down the river, giving the alarm as she went. The Sioux watched this and knowing the Pawnee forces would increase instead of diminish rallied for one last charge preparatory to final withdrawal. As they dashed against the Pawnees, who were all on foot, and were bringing their clubs and axes down with telling effect, the cry was raised among them that Red Cloud was killed. Instantly they all rushed to the spot where he had fallen from his horse, and two of them raised him up. Quickly tying his blanket around him just under his arms, they mounted their horses, and taking hold of each end of the blanket they dragged him from the field, their retreat being covered by the remainder of the party.

When they had reached a place of safety, they stopped and examined their fallen chieftain and found that though almost lifeless he was not dead. He had been shot with an arrow through the right side just below the ribs, and the point of the arrow was protruding through the skin of his back, the whole shaft lying in the wound. The arrow was dexterously removed by one of the older men, and the blood flowed freely for a time. Water was brought from a rivulet nearby, Red Cloud was given a drink, and his face and wound were bathed. After a little he began to rally, and by that time the guard from the top of an adjoining hill notified them that the Pawnees were coming up the river to the attacked village but that none of them had as yet passed the village as if to give chase to their party.

The Sioux made all haste that they could under the circumstances. Two of them continued to bathe Red Cloud's wound, while others of the party cut some saplings and prepared a travois and attached it to a gentle horse. A mat of bark and rawhide ropes was used to connect the poles, and over this was placed robes and blankets. Some green boughs were placed at the head as a protection from the sun, and on this Red Cloud laid after several wet bandages had been placed about his wound. Traveling slowly but stealthily during the remainder of the day and for some time after it had become dark, the party stopped only at intervals where there was water for the purpose of attending to the patient's wounds. During the night Red Cloud's comfort was looked after continually by watchers, and next morning he had revived sufficiently to be able to eat a little. As the next day's travel took them beyond all possible danger of being molested by their enemies, the Sioux traveled a little slower and went into camp whenever Red Cloud expressed a desire to do so.[3] The party was fifteen days retracing their line of march home, and after their arrival Red Cloud remained a very sick man for two moons, and, while he finally regained his strength and vigor, that wound has continued to trouble him at intervals ever since the time it was inflicted.

8

Marriage

MARRIAGE CUSTOMS AMONG the Lakotas in Red Cloud's
time involved a transfer of property, usually horses, from
the groom to the bride's family. The result became as
much an alliance between families as the joining of two
individuals.[1] From the following account, Red Cloud
seems to have weighed his choices carefully when the time
came to propose. His decision, made not on the field of
battle but in the domestic comfort of his village, resulted
in one of his most poignant—and tragic—stories. Surprisingly, the narrative paints a picture of Red Cloud that
is neither glowing nor laudatory, but only all too human.

Neglecting the details of married life is a common
feature of male Native American autobiographies.[2] After
Pretty Owl's dramatic entrance in his life, Red Cloud
hardly ever mentions his wife again in this narrative. Her
absence is unfortunate because this union endured for a
half century, and she receives little mention elsewhere in
the historical record.

⟿

On the broad plateau at the base of a cluster of high, bronze-colored mountains known as Raw Hide Buttes, where the waters of the North Platte River come rushing down through the narrow channel they have worn through the rocks until the walls stand perpendicular at a height of one hundred feet on either side, here where the river winds through a valley covered with wild blue grass stood the Oglala village. Great clusters and rows of lodges, some white, some touched with age and smoke, others decorated with gaudily painted suns, moons, stars, horses, and other designs of savage art, the large soldier lodge wherein the council met to which all news is brought and from which information bearing the stamp of tribal authority is disseminated, all these combined to form a picture pleasing to gaze upon.

The occupants of the village doubtless felt more at home in this locality than in any of their numerous camping places, for Fort Laramie contained within its adobe walls much of what the Indians of those days looked upon as rare luxuries. This old post situated within a few miles of the village was established in 1822 [actually 1834] by the American Fur Company and in 1849 was purchased by the government and converted into a military fort, but notwithstanding its change of ownership it continued for many years to hold its prestige as a Mecca for all the Indians of the central northwest.[3] It was in this vicinity that

the traveler could find the Sioux, Arapahos, and Cheyennes all living peaceably as neighbors, and occasionally a
village of Crows pitched their tipis here when treaties
with the tribes above mentioned permitted them. These
treaties were generally of short duration, however, and
their sojourning in close proximity of each other generally resulted in a row and a hurried flight of one tribe or
the other.

Red Cloud, having been at home for some time and
having joined in all the revelries incident to his arrival
and having told and retold the story of his latest adventure to admiring listeners both in and out of the soldier
lodge, now began to consider his private affairs. It would
have been strange indeed if a man of his standing in the
tribe could have failed to attract the favorable attention
of the young women of the village and their mothers. To
say that he was not slighted in this particular is stating
the fact mildly. Like many other young men of his age his
mind often reverted to the serious contemplation of
matrimony, and, like others also, he had his choices,
for in accordance with the privileges granted him by
the custom of his people, he chose two at least and
more if he felt disposed to pay for and provide for them.
He had long been in love with two young women who
reciprocated his affection. Pretty Owl and Pine Leaf
were their names, and the only matter for him to decide was, which of the two should be number one, for,
while he could properly marry each of them, he could
not marry both of them at once. There would have to
be two wedding ceremonies with at least a month or
two of time intervening.

On this weighty subject Red Cloud's cogitations resulted in the choosing of Pretty Owl as the first of the two to be wedded. This course once decided upon the information was imparted to his relatives who began to prepare for the event, the women by constructing a lodge of tanned elk skins and his older male relatives by conducting the negotiations with the family of Pretty Owl, which were finally concluded by presenting her parents with twelve ponies. This ceremony was carried through in the following manner: About ten o'clock in the morning of the appointed day four good horses were taken to the lodge of Pretty Owl's parents and tethered nearby. No sooner had this been done than it attracted the attention of the passersby, and soon the gossips were chattering and watching for the splendid matrimonial gift to be accepted, but, after the horses had stood until noon without any of the objects of the lodge paying the slightest attention to them, the people began to wonder at the cause of the rejection. Then the young man came dashing up to the lodge leading four more horses better than the first and dismounting tied them with the rest and rode away. The people now began to strain their eyes for a look at the lucky young woman who could command such a price, but the hours wore away, and they grew weary and went on their way. Others came to fill their places, and still the wonder grew. Predictions of a final and complete rejection of Red Cloud's suit were made, and the reasons and causes therefore volunteered. Many complained of the perverseness of Pretty Owl—for it was now known that she was the chosen one. Red Cloud was called a fool, who could do better for a less number of horses.

Thus comment continued, keeping pace with the time until near the middle of the afternoon when the young man on horseback again appeared leading four more horses far superior to the ones he had previously brought. In fact the assembled spectators readily recognized among them one of Red Cloud's favorite race horses.

Then astonishment knew no bounds. These horses were left with the other eight making twelve in all, and, shortly after they were left and the young man who brought them had gone, Pretty Owl and her father came out of the lodge. After looking over the animals in a casual manner for a few minutes, Pretty Owl began to untie them. Then arose a shout of applause from the throng of bystanders.

The next morning arrangements were made for the usual marriage festival which consisted of feasting and the performance of a dance in which only the women took part. In this dance the women and children form a large circle in the center of which four or five drummers are beating the drum while others are cooking and dishing out soup and meat to the persons composing the circle. These, as soon as they had partaken of food, joined the dancers within the circle and danced until they were weary and then fell back to the circle and in a sitting posture rested and ate again.

This dance continued during the entire day. In the meantime Red Cloud's mother, assisted by other old women, had erected his lodge upon a smooth grassy plot near the river beneath a large cottonwood tree whose spreading branches and green foliage protected it from the rays of the noon-day sun. The interior furnishing of the lodge consisted of a bed made by first laying a log on either side and staying it in position by means of small pegs driven in the ground; between this and the wall was placed a quantity of small willow boughs over which were spread buffalo robes and trade blankets. At the head of the bed a tripod made of sticks about four feet in height supported a triangular shaped mat made of willows woven together and painted in different colors. Over this and suspended from the top of the tripod hung Red Cloud's war accoutrements. The remainder of the room was occupied by firewood, crude cooking utensils, and the fireplace in the center. Large sacks made of tanned elk and buffalo skins held the clothing and trinkets of the household.

All being put in order, Red Cloud and Pretty Owl, accompanied by a number of their friends, visited their new abode and made an inspection of the premises. They were thus engaged when the master of ceremonies, who had been looking for them, appeared on the scene and reminded them that the hour of proclaiming their marriage had arrived.

Accordingly, four warriors who were in readiness spread a large blanket, and, each one taking hold of a corner and holding it high in the air, Red Cloud and Pretty Owl stepped under it while the remainder of the party formed a line in the rear. The medicine man taking the lead then gave the order to march. The four warriors, each holding a corner of the blanket with one hand and a spear in the other, marched through the village, while the master of ceremony, arrayed in paint and feathers and holding a green ash wand that he used as a baton, loudly proclaimed the nuptial knot and sounded the praises of the happy pair. The ceremony was not concluded until near sundown, the progress of the march being continually interrupted by the proffered congratulations of friends.

To this, as to each previous demonstration relating to the wedding, there was one grim and silent witness who stood aloof with jealous, scornful looks. It was Pine Leaf. No one seemed to have noticed at the time that she failed to partake of the general good feeling except Red Cloud himself, whose eagle eye caught sight of her upon several occasions during the day. Realizing that she was not aware of either his feelings or his intentions, he mentally resolved to seek her out at the first opportunity and acquaint her with his purpose, but the opportunity never came.

After the pageant had ended, Red Cloud and Pretty Owl separated, the former going to the lodge of Little Bad Wolf and Pretty Owl to her father's lodge, but, when the shades of night began to spread over the village, Red Cloud repaired to his new home and kindled a fire. Shortly afterwards his most intimate friends began to assemble, and, as darkness fell, a small procession composed entirely of women approached the lodge singing and bearing torches. These were the personal friends and relatives of Pretty Owl, and they were carrying her in a blanket supported by six buxom lasses. When they came to the lodge, the flap of the door having been thrown back for the occasion, they entered and deposited their burden at the feet of her husband, who, in playful imitation of "counting coo" [coup] on an enemy, struck her with the ramrod of his rifle exclaiming "You are mine." This ended the ceremony, and Pretty Owl at once began her household duties by preparing supper for their mutual friends, who remained and spent the evening with them.

Early the next morning as the clear sky and fading stars told the dawn of day, Red Cloud arose and getting his rope prepared to start to the hills after his horses. After going out of the lodge he turned to the right, intending to pass between it and the large tree that stood near, but he suddenly stopped. A sight of appalling horror confronted him. There in the gray of the morning with a rope about her neck, one end of which was attached to a low projecting branch of the tree, was the form of Pine Leaf, her face distorted and her open eyes resting upon Red Cloud in the glassy haze of death.[4] Quickly pulling his blanket over his head and face, he turned and hurried to the lodge of Little Bad Wolf. After telling his mother and sister of what had occurred, he threw himself face downward upon the bed and remained there as one stupefied during the rest of the day.

Soon the crying, groaning, and shrieking told that the news had spread over the village. Pretty Owl had hurriedly fled to her father, while Pine Leaf's relatives, who had arrived at the scene of death, razed Red Cloud's lodge to the ground and broke, cut, and tore into shreds its covering. But that the friends of the newly married couple mingled with the mourners, quietly picked up the most valuable of these household effects, and preserved them all, all of them would have been destroyed. Not an effort was made to stay the mad fury of Pine Leaf's enraged and excited relatives, but, as it gradually spent itself, some of the cooler ones were made acquainted with the cause and all the circumstances connected with the tragedy, which showed plainly that it was a case of suicide. Then comparative quiet was restored, and the body which had been taken down was prepared for burial.

About a mile from the village on the top of a high hill four crotched posts were placed in the ground, the crotches about six feet from the earth. In these were laid other poles forming a scaffold. About the middle of the afternoon the procession started for the grave. The litter holding the corpse was placed on a travois to which was attached an old gentle pony led by an old woman; behind this followed first the mother, leading Pine Leaf's favorite pony and accompanied by her other daughters, all of them weeping and with their hair cut short as an evidence of deep mourning. After these came the father and brothers with their hair hanging loosely over their faces which were painted black and their bodies cut and gashed. They each carried their weapons and frequently fired to the right or left crying and yelling in a hideous manner. Behind these came many other mourners, each vying with the other in making the most noise.

When the grave was reached, the litter containing the corpse was placed upon a scaffold, and provisions and utensils containing water were put there beside it. Then the dead girl's favorite pony was led up to the grave and shot. Having thus furnished her with provisions, water, and mode of conveyance in the future world, a small tanned skin lodge was spread over the whole scaffold. The party slowly and sorrowfully returned to the village. After a brief period had been courteously allowed the relatives of Pine Leaf in which to indulge their grief, they hastened to replace the losses that Red Cloud had sustained by providing him another lodge and paying him a number of horses. This occurrence made an impression upon Red Cloud that caused him to resolve never to have but one wife, and he never did.[5]

Failure

BLACK EAGLE, RED CLOUD'S NEMESIS who figured so prominently in the fifth chapter, returns in this story. Also emerging is a more mature, politically savvy Red Cloud, who displays considerable deftness in dealing with a village rival, a skill that served him well for the rest of his career.

White Horse, Red Cloud's eyes and ears on the failed raid, mentions in passing that the party encountered Mexican traders in Crow lands. Although this may sound extraordinary, aggressive traders from the longtime Spanish settlements in the Santa Fe area had made excursions to the Plains and the Rockies for decades. Crows, Cheyennes, Lakotas, and other tribes were as acquainted with fine Mexican silverwork and blankets as they were with American guns and liquor.[1]

The terminology Allen uses to describe religious matters here—"mystery mongers," "savage ignorance," "weird and grotesque superstitions," and "dark rites"— say more about Allen than Red Cloud.

The fore part of the summer had now passed; the village had long since resumed its customary appearance and its inhabitants their wonted routine of life. War parties had been leaving and returning to the village, but Red Cloud seemed to resist the temptation to join in the hunt for the enemy and contented himself with the excitement incident to the buffalo chase and with his domestic felicity. Many of his followers became restless and chafed at his seeming indifference to their accustomed practices.

Black Eagle was not slow in taking advantage of this feeling of discontent and resolved to make up a war party of which he should be the leader and whose achievements should outshine those of the much talked of Red Cloud. Starting out with this idea he succeeded after much persuasion and delay in getting ten volunteers including an old medicine man who was to juggle the fates into compliance with their most exaggerated wishes.[2] As the arrangements were being made to start, Black Eagle was desirous of increasing the number of his party but was unable to do so. This was on account of the general lack of confidence in his ability and judgement and partly because of his incautious insinuations derogatory to Red Cloud which had enraged the opposition of the latter's friends who were all powerful in the village.

The fact of Black Eagle having displayed the enmity

that he had nourished since the episode in the Big Horn Mountains caused Red Cloud to make a politic move that he might not otherwise have done. Black Eagle had been using all his persuasive powers on an Indian named White Horse in hopes of getting him to join his party but without avail. The day before the party was to start, Red Cloud quietly sent for White Horse, who was one of his trusted friends and after a long confidential talk between the two White Horse returned to his lodge with the intention of accompanying the party and keeping his eyes and ears open in Red Cloud's interest.

That night Red Cloud made it convenient to have a private interview with the old medicine man whose mysterious powers Black Eagle depended upon for unparalleled success. Red Cloud never employed these mystery mongers to accompany him on any of his exploits, for like Napoleon he believed in the strongest battalions first and the god of battles afterwards. He relied wholly upon judgement and management, tact, stratagem, and nerve. Yet it would be stating too much to say that, reared as he had been in an atmosphere of savage ignorance and weird and grotesque superstitions, he was entirely free from the influence of medicine men of the tribe. But whatever may have been his objections to them and their dark rites, he shows now a sensitive delicacy of feeling in not expressing them. At any rate, his long talk with this particular doctor of occult science resulted in the doctor quietly obtaining a proprietary interest in one of the best horses in Red Cloud's herd, to be delivered upon his return from the Black Eagle expedition.

The next morning the party left the village and traveled northwest up the Platte Valley, expecting to scout for the Crows when they reached their country.

A few days after the departure of Black Eagle and his party, Red Cloud and four others took a short hunting trip in the mountains near Laramie Peak in search of elk, deer, and other game and were quite successful, this section at that time abounding in all kinds of game. They were encamped on one of the clear mountain streams that wind among the rocks and pines and empty into the Little Laramie River. The trees about their camp were heavily hung with the meat of elk, deer, and mountain sheep, while ribs and other choice bits were roasting before the fire, around which the hunters were smoking and chatting, when suddenly their attention was called to the cracking of a bush on the creek shore near them. Supposing it was an intrusive mountain lion in quest of food, they all picked up their guns and started cautiously for the intruder. The brush formed an obstruction to their view, and they had gone but a short distance when upon the edge of a grassy opening they confronted a huge grizzly bear that was making his way leisurely toward the fresh meat of the camp. Instantly the guns were at the shoulders of the hunters, but Red Cloud stopped them, seeing at a glance that a close conflict with a grizzly between the walls of a rocky gorge not over one hundred feet apart would be unnecessarily dangerous. Accordingly at his suggestion they climbed up the sides of the gorge, two on one side and three on the other. The bear, regarding their movements for a moment, moved on toward the camp in an unconcerned manner.

Red Cloud instructed his companions to keep on the side of the rocks and hurry on down to a point opposite the camp and fire when he gave them the signal. These instructions given he moved along the side of the canyon, keeping pace with the bear whose course he could trace by the moving of the brush. Presently the bear reached the opening in which the camp was situated, and Red Cloud gave the signal to fire. The hunters who were scattered along the sides of the hills on each side of the camp could not all get sight of the animal on account of the intervening trees and brush, but Red Cloud and one other fired. The result was as Red Cloud had foreseen— a wounded bear made ferocious by the pain inflicted, kicking and tearing at everything in sight.

Presently another shot was fired, and then another, each one having the effect of increasing the animal's fury until finally it rolled to the ground dead. Then the hunters came down to their camp cautiously, laden with rocks which they threw at the carcass as they approached to assure themselves that the bear was dead. Their success elated them greatly, for the killing of a bear is considered no small achievement by the Indians who look upon Bruin as a sort of medicine animal and the king of all beasts.[3]

Nearly two weeks had elapsed since the departure of Black Eagle and his party. The little band of hunters had returned from their hunt laden with fresh meat, and Red Cloud was the proud possessor of a new bear robe. The cool, early autumn days were spent in horse racing and other sports and the nights in feasting and dancing the Omaha dance. This dance is usually performed in a lodge erected for the purpose and owned by a society that exerts quite an influence over the conduct of its members and through them the affairs of the tribe. The dance is participated in only by men and boys dressed in their gaudiest costumes, and it is remarkable only for the accurate time they keep with each other and the monotonous thump of the drum and the old see-saw song of the drummers.[4]

Thus time was passing on without much note being taken of its departure, when one bright afternoon in September a party was sighted near the village; some of them were on horseback, but more of them were on foot. Some Indians who had been out in that direction on horseback came in and reported that it was Black Eagle's party returning, and it was evident they were coming back in distress.

As the party moved very slowly and were some distance away when they were sighted, the sun was nearly down when they entered the village footsore and weary. Their relatives set up a mourning wail at the sight of their destitute condition, and they were immediately taken and cared for. Although defeated, they were still heroes in the estimation of their friends and families. During the evening the several members of Black Eagle's party were invited out to dine and tell the story of their trip. Black Eagle also recounted the story of his adventure in the Soldier Lodge in order that it might become the property of the public as soon as possible. Red Cloud, painted and wrapped in his blanket, with his face covered beyond recognition, was a listener to these recitals, but, long after the fires had died out in most of the lodges and the embers that transmitted a pale reflection to the walls of the thick elk skin lodge were all that remained of his own evening fire, Red Cloud sat in deep meditation awaiting the arrival of a visitor.

Presently the flap that answered for a door to the lodge was raised, and White Horse entered. After the two had exchanged greetings and White Horse had seated himself upon a buffalo mat, he began the discourse.

"My brother," he said, "I am come to tell you of our unfortunate trip. I have told it many times tonight, and doubtless you have heard it over and over again; perhaps you have heard me recite it, but, if so, you have probably guessed that I was not telling a true story." Here the lighted pipe was handed to him, and he paused and took a whiff or two, as if to recall the actual events that had transpired and to separate them from the chaff that had been related by agreement. Then resuming, he said, "The next day after we left here we came upon the big trails that the white men have made on their journey to the great ocean, and, as it leads in the direction of the Crow country, we concluded to follow it, which we did for four days. Nothing of importance as yet occurred, only the usual traveling and camping, and then traveling again.

"On the evening of the fifth day after leaving here we met a party of Mexicans returning to their home in the South. They had wagons that were empty, and we found that they had been on a trading expedition to the Crows. We decided to stay with them that night. They had a few Navajo blankets left, for which we exchanged some dry meat and an extra horse or two without letting them know the object of our visit to the Crows. We learned that the Crow village was encamped on the head of Bad Water.

"When we stopped at noon the next day, the old medicine man unpacked his horse at a short distance from the rest of us and seemed sullen and refused to eat or talk. I saw him take a small bag from his pack and start uphill near the camp. Shortly afterward I left the camp also and reached a point from which I could plainly watch his actions. I saw him take four small rocks about the size of a horse's hoof, and, after holding them up to the sun one at a time, he laid them upon the ground about two feet apart in the form of a square.[5] In the center he placed a large round flat stone; around this center stone he stuck willow wands that stood about as high as his knee. The tops of these sticks were wrapped with red and blue and yellow cloths that I suppose contained some kind of medicine. After this had been done, he brought the top ends of the wands together and fastened them. He then began whittling tobacco and roots and pulverizing them with his hands and placed the stuff on the flat rock. Then he took his powder horn, and, after sprinkling powder from the central rock to each of the four smaller ones, this done he took out his flint and steel and a piece of dry and rotten wood. After firing one end of the wood he began to hum a low song and to move in a circle about the stone, holding the piece of burning wood first to the north and then to the east and then to the west and to the south and then towards the sun. Just as he was about to apply the fire to the powder on the rock lying to the north, I walked upon the scene, passing him very closely. He stopped, threw up his hands, and exclaimed, 'O my son, you have broken my medicine.' Without stopping to answer him I walked on to camp. Presently he returned and contrary to my expectations made no complaint to Black Eagle to my intrusion.

"Our party moved on in the afternoon and camped

at dark as usual without any occurrence worth noting. The next morning scouts were sent out on either side, and we continued our course up the creek. About noon our scouts returned with the information that, according to what the Mexicans had said and their own knowledge of the country, we were approaching too near the enemy in daytime and that it was but a short distance through the mountains to Bad Water where the Crows were supposed to be camped. We therefore halted, and our camp was pitched where we were hidden from view by the circling clusters of brush. Our horses were placed in a semi-circular nook of the valley that extended into the mountains and a guard placed over them.

"The afternoon was spent in eating, resting, and sleeping. During the afternoon the medicine man again went to the hills to make medicine, and again I walked through his circle, but he made no complaint in the camp. About sundown we were all astir, eating and making preparations for starting as soon as it was dark. Having finished eating before the others, I got my saddle ready for packing and went out to the herd and led in one of my horses. I left the herd grazing quietly and the guard who was on foot standing part way between the horses and the camp, watching for a signal to be given to drive in as it was growing dark.

"I had just tied my horse to a small tree when we heard the crash of stampeding horses and the whiz of flying arrows, and our herders came running into camp shouting 'Crows!'

"Everyone of us jerked our guns and dashed out and fired at them but without effect. They were all on foot and just turning the point of the hill when our shots fell among them. They were all running and swinging their blankets at the frightened herd that only awaited an opportunity that afforded it by the open valley just beyond to break into a run. Some of the Crows were deftly swinging their ropes at the heads of the horses as they crowded against the side of the hill, and two of them had made lucky throws and caught horses and were mounting them just as the rest of the horses cleared the side of the hill and fled in terror.

"Then there was a chase. After running with the party for a few minutes, I ran back and got my horse, now the only one in camp, and started in pursuit again, hoping that the herd might run into some narrow gorge that would prove impassable and thereby give us an opportunity to get back part of our horses at least. I began to think this had occurred, for just as I was nearing our party there was a rapid succession of shots and war cries. Clouds had been flitting across the face of the moon, causing it first to be light, then dark. During one of these lights, just as I turned a point of timber, I could see across the little valley in front of me, our party halted and occasionally shooting at some object upon the ground. Urging my horse on I came up to them and found they had killed a Crow and were wreaking their vengeance upon him for the losses they had sustained. I rode up and struck the body with my bow, for in the distance we could hear the sound of tramping horses, and we knew they were beyond recovery.

"After a little discussion, Black Eagle, being the leader of the party, was accorded the honor of scalping the enemy, but, just as he had unsheathed his knife and was bending over the body, the moon shone out from behind a cloud. Someone standing near the feet of the victim remarked, 'It looks as if this Crow was wearing Sioux moccasins.' Black Eagle raised his hand from the scalp lock instantly, and we looked and saw that they were of Sioux make and pattern. Someone asked for Red Deer, and there was no response; then we counted ourselves. The mutilated body of the supposed Crow was taken up and carried to the creek where the face was washed and a fire kindled by which to view it. It was the face of Red Deer who, as you know, was the swiftest runner in the tribe. His speed had carried him away from the rest so suddenly that he was not missed, and, as he came into view around one of the brushy points at a time when the light of the moon fell upon him, he was mistaken for a Crow and shot to death by his friends. His body was wrapped in the folds of blankets and robes and placed in the spreading branches of a large tree, from which we turned going heavy hearted and silent to our camp. That night the ghost of Red Deer kept calling to us from the hills until rest was impossible, and we decided to move. Accordingly we started out on foot in the direction of home. We had gone but a short distance down the creek when we came upon four horses with packs and saddles, and we took them. They were the Crow ponies that their owners had abandoned for fear of discovery and crawling past our camp had got our herd in exchange. But the old ponies proved of value to us, for we rode them turn about, which was a great relief.

"Black Eagle was sullen and cross as we rode and walked down the creek. Once he upbraided the medicine man for the worthlessness of his medicine. The old man indignantly told him that the ghost was to blame, that he made no medicine, that he had tried it twice, and that each time the ghost came and broke the spell. 'Why,' said he, 'the whole country is full of ghosts and evil spirits,' to which Black Eagle replied, 'There is one more ghost in it now than there was, that of Red Deer, and there will be one less evil spirit in it when you are out of it.' But the old man partly redeemed himself in Black Eagle's estimation when he invented the story that we all told here tonight. This is the story, Red Cloud, just as it happened, but somehow I feel bad at the death of Red Deer. I feel that my interference with the medicine of the old man was the cause of his death."

Red Cloud gave his friend good reason why he was in no way to blame, and after another smoke the young man departed.

Scalped Alive

TO ADD INSULT TO INJURY, Red Cloud followed up Black Eagle's failed raid against the Crows with an enormously profitable one of his own. Little wonder his fellow Lakotas clamored to follow this successful tactician into battle and that his adversaries among enemy tribes came to learn his name.

That Red Cloud would inadvertently confront a Blackfoot raider—a rare adversary who experienced the brunt of Red Cloud's fury and lived to tell the tale—near a Crow village is not surprising. Blackfeet war parties frequented Crow country in the 1850s.[1]

Late in the fall the Oglalas moved up the Platte River to the mouth of Deer Creek, about twenty miles above the mouth of LaPrele Creek where Fort Fetterman was afterwards established. Here they found game plenty, and they went into camp for the winter. Not long after they were established here, a wagon train loaded with trade goods came to them. After making the proper arrangement four of the traders decided to go into camp with the Oglalas, while two with four wagons went on to trade in the Crow villages in the Yellowstone country.

About four days after these wagons left the Oglala camp, Red Cloud enlisted thirteen of his friends and leaving the village in the night started out to harass the Crows and avenge the death of "High Sar" [High Star, another name of Red Deer?] in accordance with a promise he had made to White Horse, who now accompanied him. Following the trail made by the wagons, they lost no time in scouting for a village. On the evening of the first day they went into camp on the Clear Fork of Powder River near the place where the traders' wagons had camped a day or two before. After they were in camp a little while, Red Cloud went walking about over the abandoned campground of the trading party, and his quick eye soon caught sight of signs that indicated that Indians had been there too. Following that clue he soon became satisfied that a party of Crows had met the traders at this point and escorted them to their village, which he concluded could not be more than a day's travel distance.

On joining the others he made them acquainted with his discovery and opinions. After a general discussion it was agreed that the Crows must be camped somewhere in the neighborhood of Wolf Mountains. It was decided that after a short rest they would travel on, following as closely as they could the trail of the wagons by the light of the moon.

They counted, however, upon uncertainties, for about midnight it suddenly clouded up and began to snow. This left them no recourse but to hunt some sheltered spot and go into camp. They selected a narrow canyon with high rocky walls. In this they placed their horses after first ascertaining that it narrowed at the head so as to prevent them from escaping. Then making their camp at the mouth of it, they decided that, on account of the fierce blizzard that was then raging, they would be safe from any possible intrusion. Accordingly they all wrapped themselves in their robes and laid down. They were undisturbed by anything except the storm, which was still raging in the morning. This gave them an opportunity to build a small fire under the bank where they could roast their dried meat without fear of being detected by the rising smoke that would have discovered their whereabouts to any chance passerby upon a calm day. Shortly the weather cleared, and a party of four immediately left camp, one going north, one south, one east, and one to the west for the purpose of cautiously looking over the country to see what they could discover.

Before noon they all returned. None of them saw

anything except the one who went north. He had made
the important discovery of a fresh trail made that day by a
herd of horses. Following the trail in the opposite direction to that which the horses had been traveling, he came
to where they had fed overnight. Here he found moccasin
tracks made by the Crow who had driven them in. He
reported that from the size of the trail there must have
been fifty or sixty horses.

Red Cloud studied for some time. The snow was
deep, and their movements had to be made cautiously,
for their trail would be easily discovered, yet he was reasonably sure that the Crows would not be expecting a
war party during such weather. He was also confident
that they were but little distance from the Crow village,
for it is very rarely that Indians take their horses out to
grass a great distance from their camp. Finally he decided
upon a course of action. Leaving two men with the horses
he instructed them to have all saddled and to break them
plenty [of] cottonwood boughs on which to feed during
the time they might have to rest. The rest of the party
then started on foot up the gulch to the point where the
Crow herd had crossed it. They traveled in single file in
order to leave as small a trail as possible. They reached
the objective point about noon, and Red Cloud figured
that it would soon be time for the Crows to come out
from camp with the horses again.

He selected a thick patch of timber with a heavy
growth of underbrush, among which there was considerable dead wood and fallen timber. Taking eight of his
men he placed them in this thicket with instructions to
remain there concealed until he either came to them or

called to them. Under no circumstances were they to betray their whereabouts to the approaching enemy unless
he called to them to do so. If anyone of them disobeyed
this order, he was to be sent home alone and in disgrace.

Then leaving them he and White Horse and two others stepped into the trail made by the herd of horses in the
morning and followed it up the hill to where the horses
had been feeding in the valley before being taken away by
their owner. Here by stepping carefully from one horse
track to another they were enabled to reach a small cluster of cedars that stood at the edge of the valley without
leaving any trail. Being now in a position from which
they could see without being seen, they beat down the
snow where they were standing and waited for the arrival
of the Crow and his horses. While here Red Cloud instructed his companions in the part they were to perform, the pith of which was that they were to capture the
Crow alive if possible. Under no conditions were they to
fire upon him. They were to let him get away if they could
not get him alive.

"But how do you know that he will come?" asked
White Horse.

Red Cloud answered by calling their attention to
the fine, luxurious, dry mountain blue grass from which
the horses had pawed the snow and to the now hard
formed crust of snow that everywhere lay upon the earth.
By these tokens he wisely concluded that the Crow
would bring his horses back to where the grass was good
and easy of access, and where also they would be well
protected from a storm by the high mountains on three
sides of the valley.

And his calculations based upon his keen observations and the use of common sense proved to be correct, for it was not long before the leading horses of the herd were seen winding over the hills in their direction. Red Cloud and his companions watched and waited. The herd they could see was driven by one man on horseback. When they came near to where the eight Sioux were in hiding, Red Cloud was anxious for fear that they would in some way discover themselves to him. But after the Crow had passed them and his horses had raised the hill which placed them in the valley, he felt no more uneasiness on that score. As the horses began to snip the grass, the Crow stopped and sat for a while on his pony humming a native song. Presently he took a pair of hobbles from his saddle, and kicking his pony in the side with his head he rode straight to the cluster of cedars and dismounted. Squatting down he began putting the hobbles on his pony.

Red Cloud was about eight feet of him, but he knew that the least move would cause the snow to crack, and, notwithstanding the Crow's buffalo robe that came up over his ears, he would hear it. But that to wait until he had finished hobbling his pony was to lose the best opportunity. He slowly raised one foot, and, placing it as far in front of him as he could reach, he sprang upon him with the bound of a tiger and grasped him about the arms and body. The others who had followed instantly now had hold of him also. The dumbfounded Crow, after one gigantic struggle during which he grunted and groaned like a bear, subsided and became limp as a rag and trembled in every limb.

Red Cloud took his belt and knife and his robe and

his bow and quiver of arrows, then told him in the sign language that they were not going to kill him. This seemed to revive him greatly, and he asked by the same method what they intended doing with him. Red Cloud told him to stand up like a man if he was brave and not to make any noise, and they would send him home. Then taking the knife that he had deprived him of, he handed it to White Horse and told him in Sioux to scalp him. Red Cloud stood in front of him with his war club raised, while the other two Sioux held him on each side. White Horse, who was behind him, took hold of his long braided scalp lock. When the keen edge of the knife touched the scalp at its roots, horror was depicted in every lineament of the unfortunate victim's face. But bracing one foot in front of the other he underwent the ordeal without a struggle or a moan. When White Horse had finished his fiendish work and stepped back with a look of grim satisfaction and the Crow scalp dangling from his belt, Red Cloud rapidly told him in signs to hurry to the village and tell his people that Red Cloud and three other Sioux had done it.

Ordering the others to catch a horse each and one for him, he guarded the Crow until they were all mounted, then giving him a thin blanket in lieu of his robe, told him to go and say at the village that the only reason he spared his life was because a Crow was not worth killing.

The Crow hurried away with the blood trickling down his face and neck, and the four Sioux leisurely moved off with the herd, keeping a good watch on the form of the fast receding Crow until he was lost to view.

They then turned it about and drove it up to where the eight men were hiding. After catching each of them a horse they moved down the gulch to their camp. Here they hurriedly ate some dried meat that had been roasted for them.

Red Cloud detailed four men and told them to get their own horses and accoutrements and take the herd on toward the Platte over the trail they had come on and to travel slowly so that the rest could overtake them, telling all the others to turn the Crow horses with the herd before it drove away and to saddle their own mounts and get everything in readiness for moving. He gave orders to the two herders to take all the animals thus saddled and lead them over a small mountain to the east and remain there until they came.

These arrangements completed Red Cloud and his eight companions were once more on foot. Separating, four went among the rocks on one side of the gulch, and Red Cloud and four others took the other side, thus forming an ambush for the Crow war party that they confidently expected to pursue them. Long they waited to hear the dash of horses and the war cry of the Crows. Darkness came, however, and Red Cloud and his companions gave up their ambush and going to their horses mounted and followed on after the herd, overtaking it that night and returning to the village on the Platte without further incident.

Years later under the shadow of the great guns of Fort Benton a number of Indians of different tribes were congregated for the purpose of transacting business with the government.[2] An old Blackfoot Indian who had been recounting the above story and displaying his wound on the head to a party of listeners, among whom there were some Sioux, was told that Red Cloud, who was then at the fort, had served a Crow that way at one time. He immediately hunted Red Cloud up and thanked him for sparing his life. Red Cloud of course was astonished and asked him when and where. The Blackfoot recounted the time and place and circumstances relating to the affair, adding, "It was pretty hard to lose my scalp, but the horses I cared nothing about. They were not mine anyway. Myself and three others of my tribe had just stolen them from the Crow village which was nearly a day's travel from where you found me. Shortly after we had taken them, the big storm came, and we knew that the snow had covered our trail and that the Crows would not in all probability miss their horses, and, if they did, they could not follow us, nor guess which way we had gone. With all these circumstances in our favor, the other three went back to get some more horses under the cover of the storm and left me to watch the herd, and I had just returned from a creek over the hill where our plunder was hidden and where I had watered the horses when you jumped me. After you let me go, I went to our camp and shortly afterwards my companions returned with another herd of Crow horses. After learning what had happened, we took a northwesterly course from where you left me and hurried home as fast as possible."

The old man's accuracy in telling the story and his scalp wound convinced Red Cloud of his identity. After lighting the pipe they had a smoke and a talk over the fortunes of war.[3]

11

The Pipe Dance

By THE 1850S RED CLOUD'S STANDING as a leader was assured. The fact that his excursion against the Ute tribe of present Utah and Colorado was uneventful or that the Poncas of eastern Nebraska made a successful raid on his village apparently did nothing to diminish his stature. He needed only the affirmation of a public ceremony before the gathered tribe to confirm his prominence, and that ceremony, based on the description given here, was apparently the *Hunka*. The Hunka, with an elaborate giveaway of a wealthy person's possessions as its climax, signified the exalted position Red Cloud and his children held among the Oglalas.[1]

According to Charles P. Jordan, a longtime white friend of Red Cloud, the husband of one of Red Cloud's nieces, and a credible biographical source, Red Cloud's marriage occurred sometime between 1848 and 1851. A Red Cloud family genealogy, in the form of an heirship affidavit held by the South Dakota State Historical Society, states that his first daughter, Wears War Bonnet (later Julia Long

Soldier) was born about 1850. Four other daughters followed; the youngest, Tells Him, later Fannie Chase Alone, was born about 1860. The birth year of Red Cloud's son Jack appears in the following story as 1852. From the information on Jack's tombstone, however, the year of his birth would be about 1858. Once again, the reader must be extremely cautious when considering the dates assigned in the Red Cloud narrative.[2]

⟨≈⟩

During the next five years Red Cloud's operations were confined mostly to affairs pertaining to the village and his own family, which now consisted of his wife and three children, his oldest girl born in 1850 and his son Jack in 1852 and another daughter born in 1854. Aside from the regular hunting expeditions engaged in during this period, Red Cloud in company with a few others made one long journey to the Ute country in the wintertime, but after enduring numerous hardships returned without having seen an enemy.

The village camped on the Niobrara River near where Fort Niobrara is now situated in the fall of 1854 and remained there until the following spring.[3] While here the Sioux received a very sudden and surprising call from their old enemies, the Poncas, who dashed through their village killing two Sioux and running off quite a number of horses. They were hotly pursued but not overtaken. Shortly afterwards the village moved north to White River to a point about one hundred miles from its confluence with the Missouri. All the different bands of the Oglalas were present in this village except the Cut Off band, which still held its sway further south.[4]

It was in this that Red Cloud decided to have the Pipe Dance Rite conferred upon himself and family. Tribal customs at this time made it necessary that this be done in order that they might enjoy all the privileges possible to obtain from a crude but domineering aboriginal aristocracy, consisting of the chiefs and their families.[5] Red Cloud had long been a great warrior and for years had been the head soldier of the Indian soldiers, but he was not a chief nor was he eligible to a chieftaincy until he and his family had had the Pipe Dance Rite performed in their honor. From the sons thus honored were the chiefs chosen, while the female members of these families were recognized as the sisters, wives, and mothers of chiefs.

In olden times the custom of confining their marriages to their own class was imperative, and in this the evidence of the similarity of human nature again presents itself, for the Indians, the most democratic people in the world, had their little schemes devised, and in admirable working order, for the purpose of dividing their people into classes. Like other similar schemes, in order that it might not be detected as a glaring fraud, the entrance to the favored circle was guarded by an admission so large that none but the wealthiest could afford the expense. As a consequence there existed a comparatively small class who were eligible to the right to rule. Recognizing this fact and seeing the advantage of entering, instead of opposing this select circle, Red Cloud, having grown wealthy as well as great, decided to enter.

As stated before the admission fee was high, not only requiring the applicant, in most instances, to give up everything he possessed in way of robes and horses, which at that time constituted their wealth. But the mere fact of an Indian being willing to do this was not sufficient, he must be investigated, and the fact must be established that he is possessed of a considerable quantity of such wealth, before his application will be considered. It can readily be seen that this scheme worked like a charm; the mass were excluded from the benefit of the rite, but not from the exercises, for it was one of their institutions. It was their day, and a gala day it was; feasting and dancing had no bounds upon such occasions. All could be spectators to the ceremony who chose, for it was performed openly and in the following manner, several days having been spent in preparation as to the provisions for feasting and so on.

At a given time all the chiefs and sacred men, not doctors but another class of medicine men, assemble at the chosen spot where the huge post has been set firmly in the ground extending to a height of three feet above the earth. Around this post, which is the altar, the spectators form a circle, leaving an amphitheater in the center of sufficient size. Within the east half of this opening the chiefs and sacred men take their positions. The candidates are placed in the west half of the opening in a row a few feet back from the altar.

When everything is in readiness, the chiefs going in single file pass in front of the candidates. As they do so, each chief lays his hand upon the head of each candidate. Then marching back to their positions, as many chiefs as there are candidates again go forward bearing each a vessel filled with water, with which they wash the candidates' faces, then their hands and feet.

When this operation has been finished and the chiefs have taken their positions, the first sacred man moves slowly toward the altar, making strange pantomimes with a large eagle feather. When he comes to the altar, he pauses and lays his right hand upon it. He raises his eyes and left hand to the sun and vows to the Great Spirit that he is a pure man, emphasizing his idea of what constitutes purity by adding that he has never lied to the injury of his people and that he has never spilled the blood of any of his tribe and that all can believe in him in whatever he does.

After having imparted this information to the Great Spirit and the audience, he goes to the first candidate, and, after taking a small bag from his belt, he proceeds to paint his face. After he has displayed his decorative skill on the first candidate and has moved to the next for the same purpose, another sacred man comes to the altar in the same manner and after registering the same vow and giving the same explanation proceeds to candidate number one and begins painting his arms and hands. Then there follows another priest who after paying his respects to the Great Spirit and a tribute to himself at the altar proceeds to paint the legs of the candidate from the knees down to the feet. Then follows another who pours oil upon their heads, after which comes the High Priest who after taking his vow at the altar proceeds to talk to the back seats by lecturing the candidates upon the duty they owe to their people and the great responsibility they have assumed by virtue of their exalted position.

When he finishes his lecture, he beckons for the chiefs, who come forward. Each adult candidate is taken by the hand by a chief, and each child candidate is taken upon the back of a chief. Together they move in a circle about the altar, while the High Priest chants a refrain to the Great Spirit. At the conclusion of this exercise he takes a bunch of small, downy, white eagle feathers, taken from under the eagle's wings, and fastening one upon each of the candidates' heads as a badge of honor, pronounces them of the chiefs. They are conducted to the east half of the circle where they take their places among their peers.

Then a select few of the best dancers of the tribe are ushered into the west half of the circle where they furnish an entertainment for a short time in honor of the newly created chiefs at the close of which congratulations and feasting are in order. And it was such a ceremony that Red Cloud and his family passed through upon their native Dakota heath in the summer of 1855.

To Whip a Dog

SOME OF THE NEXT STORY'S elements would have sounded
familiar to Charles Allen. His years in Indian country gave
Allen ample opportunity to witness buffalo hunts and
the preparation of robes. Also, in the 1870s he had seen
for himself the depth and strength of the political alliance between the Lakotas and Cheyennes, which was
routinely evident in the 1850s.[1]

Less familiar to Allen may have been the punishment
Red Cloud inflicted upon an unlucky Cheyenne man.
Evidently Red Cloud helped take on the responsibility of
keeping good order in his village. He may have belonged
to the select male society of "soldiers" or "marshals" called
the *akicita*, whose members traditionally were enjoined
to maintain appropriate conduct within the camp. They
oftentimes supervised the seeming chaos of village moves
and communal buffalo hunts. Their means of punishing
offenders included physical beatings and property destruction. No resident was above their dictates.[2]

In the early fall the Oglalas moved to Powder River and began their annual hunt for winter robes and meat. Red Cloud with a party of fifteen families, including his own, camped on the Clear Fork, while other small parties went out in other directions to establish hunting camps, their camps upon such occasions being usually placed in an opening in the thickest timber they could find in order that their presence might not frighten the buffalo.

Among Red Cloud's party were about forty hunters, most of whom were provided with the then popular Hawkins rifle. They first began the hunt by going out twenty or thirty miles with their extra pack ponies and remaining two or three days or until they had secured meat and hides enough to complete their pack. Then they would return to their family camp and after resting themselves and horses for a day go back to the hunting field.

In these hunts they would approach the game by crawling as near as possible before firing, thus enabling them to make dead shots. Their camp on these hunts would be any place where night happened to overtake them, and the choice bits of meat and marrow taken from the buffalo and roasted before the fire would constitute their daily food. After hunting in this manner for awhile the buffalo would become too wild to be approached on foot. Then they would change their tactics and commenced killing them by the chase.

After sighting a herd they would manage to get on the opposite side to the wind. By riding very slowly toward it they were usually enabled to get quite close before the animals took alarm, but, as soon as they threw up their heads and began to move, then the charge was made, and the chase begun. Mounted upon their fastest horses they would run in among the buffalo and picking out one each would follow it closely, shooting it as fast as they could reload, if necessary, but as a rule the first shot would be sufficient.

Another plan that they worked to advantage when all the conditions were favorable was to get a herd upon some high level tableland and surrounding it on all sides, except the one in the direction they wished it to go, then giving them a scare, would run them over a steep precipice. As buffalo were like sheep, in that where the leader went they all tried to follow, they were enabled to kill hundreds of them by driving them to their own destruction before the main body of the herd would turn and break away through the ranks of their pursuers.

When such an undertaking was accomplished, as it frequently was, the Indians would all move to some creek nearest to the slaughter and begin the manufacture of robes and drying of meat on a large scale. The robes were tanned first by stretching them upon the ground and pinning down the outer edges, making them firm. Then a fleshing knife, a small steel tool crooked something like a hoe, was used to remove what particles of flesh were left upon the hide when it was removed from the animal. In early days before such knives were obtainable, a part of an elk antler was used, one prong forming the handle and the other dressed down to an edge forming the blade. With these instruments the hide was thoroughly scraped; then a mixture of buffalo brains and liver was applied to the flesh side of the hide and was left in the sun to absorb the mixture, which had the effect of cutting the gluey substance and penetrating the pores of the skin. When the hide had lain a sufficient length of time in the sun, it was washed until it became soft. Then two hides thus prepared were taken and spread with their flesh sides placed together and left overnight in order that all the moisture might be absorbed and evenly distributed through the skins making them limp and pliable.

Then the frame was made of small poles, in the same manner that quilting frames are constructed with the exception that the robe frames were set up in a perpendicular position by placing the ends of two of the poles in the ground. In this frame the hides were securely fastened and stretched taut by means of rawhide thongs strung around the edge of the hide and lashed about the poles. While in the frame it was scraped from time to time with the fleshing knife and kept soft by the application of the preparation of buffalo brains which were rubbed in until the surface became dry. Then it was thoroughly rubbed with sandstone or a large porous bone of a buffalo or some other large animal. When this operation had been performed a number of times, it was taken from the frame and drawn around a taut rope or a small sapling in a see-saw manner until it becomes soft and pliable, and the process of tanning was complete and a finished robe the result.

This fall hunt of the Oglalas proved very successful.

They secured a great many robes, and a large quantity of meat was dried for winter use. As was agreed upon before separating, the various hunting parties congregated at a point down the Powder River about three days' travel from their hunting grounds, where they established their winter camp. Later on a Cheyenne village moved to the river and camped about a mile below them. Word had been sent to Fort Laramie by both villages as to their location, so that the traders would have no difficulty in finding them, for they had now learned to look forward to their winter's trade with the whites as something wholly indispensable.

The winter passed without any incident worth recording, except perhaps a little altercation that Red Cloud had with one of the Cheyenne warriors. Red Cloud was proverbially kind to the women of his tribe and notably considerate for their welfare upon all occasions. Therefore, when a Sioux woman came to him one day crying and told him the story of the abuse she had been subjected to by a Cheyenne, Red Cloud, after first ascertaining the identity and exact location of the offender, called seven of his trusted friends and requested them to follow him and started for the Cheyenne village.

A few of the headmen and chiefs in those days carried sabers that had either been picked up on some military camping ground or presented to them by an officer at some of the posts. Red Cloud in addition to his gun was armed with one of these weapons. Upon arriving at the lodge of the Cheyenne he told his followers to remain outside and prevent interference; then he entered the Cheyenne's lodge and finding him in immediately began beating him over the head with his saber.

The noise that the two men made in their struggle soon began to attract the attention of the other Cheyennes, who began at once to gather towards the lodge. They were very much surprised when they saw that it was surrounded by a few Sioux who were motioning them to keep back in a very threatening manner. They managed to hold the Cheyennes at a distance until Red Cloud, who had beaten his man in a manner he considered satisfactory, emerged from the lodge. In the sign language he told the astonished Cheyennes that he did not come to their village to fight them, that he only came down to whip a dog. As he had accomplished the object of his visit, he would now go home.

So saying he turned and with his party left the village unmolested. This feat of Red Cloud's was looked upon by the rest of the Indians, both Sioux and Cheyenne, as an astonishing procedure inasmuch as Indians very rarely engage in personal encounters for the settlements of difficulties. As a rule when they are angry enough to fight, they are angry enough to kill, and for the further reason that the Cheyennes were known by all the tribes and all plainsmen to be second to no Indians in bravery and the execution of bold and desperate undertakings. They would in war come nearer taking even chances than any other Indians of the plains, most of whom depended entirely on advantages gained by cunning and stratagem. Why they should permit one of their number to be beaten nearly to death in their own village could be accounted for in no way except by reason that the deed was done by Red Cloud, the great chief of the Sioux, whom they knew to harm meant war.

Decoying the Crows

RED CLOUD FOLLOWS UP a lengthy account of tricking a Crow raiding party with a brief mention of an uncharacteristic setback. Interestingly, he mentions Young Man Afraid of His Horse, the father of whom was considered the head chief of the Oglalas. Red Cloud, no matter his exploits, would never achieve the status equal to that the tribe conferred on Man Afraid and later on his son. Heredity and family history, as much as their personal achievements, determined their social position. Red Cloud's allusion to the younger man's success—a triumph that reinforced Young Man Afraid's destiny as an Oglala leader—in nearly the same breath as mention of his own failure hints at a long-standing rivalry between them.[1]

⟨ornament⟩

In the summer of 1856 the Oglalas moved by easy stages north and east to a point on the Little Missouri River about fifty miles south of where Fort Buford was located on the Yellowstone. They had been in a state of comparative peace with the tribes on the west of them for a good many months and in consequence released to a considerable degree their usual vigilance. It was not long until they had reason to regret it, for after spending a few days in hunting, racing, and feasting in their new location they woke up one morning to find that the cunning Crows had paid them a visit and taken many of their horses. A party of fifteen or twenty was organized to pursue them and started upon the Crow trail at once with Red Cloud as leader.[2]

After traveling for two days west and south they reached the mouth of Tongue River. Here they rested that night and the next day, sending out scouts in the meantime to search for the Crow village. In the evening these scouts returned with the intelligence that there was a small village of about twenty lodges camped at the mouth of Rosebud Creek, a distance of one night's march up the Yellowstone.

Accordingly, as soon as it was dark, the Sioux resumed their journey, following up the south side of the Yellowstone River. Both they and their horses having been greatly refreshed by the long rest they had taken, they were enabled to make good time. A little before daylight they arrived as close to the Crow village as they cared to get until daylight should give them an opportunity to size up the situation.

They had not long to wait, for with the first streak of day came a perfect view of the lodges, which were few in number as their guides had told them, and a fair sweeping view of creek and river valleys beyond showed them that there were no other villages near. Presently the Crows began to start out after their horses. The Sioux, watching the direction in which most of them went, had no difficulty in determining where most of the horses were located and accordingly began circling around the village through the hills at a pace that would enable them to reach the herds about the time the Crows were gathering up their respective bunches.

Dividing into parties of two and three, the Sioux charged the Crows, who were scattered and on foot and killed and scalped three of them before they realized their danger. Then taking several bunches of horses aggregating about two hundred head and driving them to a common center, they stampeded them in the direction they wished to go. The Crows were taken at a disadvantage; they had to drive horses into camp before a party could be mounted of sufficient strength to follow. By the time this was effected, the Sioux had a long distance the better of them.

Seeing that they were being pursued by a small party of Crows, Red Cloud resorted to a ruse that effectually checked their advance. Stopping the herd in a deep hollow the Sioux changed horses as quickly as possible. Then directing five of their number to proceed with the herd in a slow trot, he took the remainder of his men and followed slowly, covering their retreat by winding around the base of the hills and through ravines in such a manner as to keep out of sight of the pursuing Crows and thereby suggesting to them that an ambush had been prepared for their benefit. This had the desired effect, for as soon as the Crows discovered that the stolen herd was moving slowly and that it was being driven by a few Sioux when there had been many, they stopped the pursuit, fearing an ambush. The Sioux moved on to their village on the Little Missouri River with about twice as many horses as they had lost.

Soon after they had returned to camp, a big council was held for the purpose of discussing the situation. It was nearing the season of the year when it would be necessary to engage in the fall hunt, and to accomplish this they would have to scatter out as usual. At these times they rather preferred to be at peace with the neighboring tribes. They knew of course that other tribes had to make their fall hunts as well as themselves, but they knew also that there would be enough young warriors among the Crows not needed in the chase to make it very unpleasant for a small camp of Sioux should they decide to retaliate, as they most likely would.

After the question had been discussed pro and con, Red Cloud proposed the following plan, which was adopted. The whole village was to divide into small family groups as usual for the purpose of scattering out to hunt. Before starting, however, two warriors with their wives and lodge were to volunteer from each group. If they had children, they were to be sent with their relations, but the warriors were to remain in the vicinity of the old camp to receive the Crows, who would, it was thought, make their appearance there before looking for the Sioux elsewhere. Each warrior was to keep very little plunder and only two good horses, a mount for himself and wife. These were to be kept closely hobbled in the daytime and tied to the lodges at night.

The Sioux at that time had a bad custom of disposing of their worthless horses. That is, when an animal became crippled or too old and worn out to be of any further use to them, they would take it to some out-of-the-way spot where there was good grass and water and give it the privilege of remaining unmolested until it died. This they termed "giving it to the moon."

Therefore, upon this occasion as a further protection to the warriors who were to remain behind, each hunting group was called upon to take a close inventory of all the animals in their respective herds that should be "given to the moon." In this manner a herd of about sixty old hacks were gathered together that made quite a respectable appearance when seen feeding at a distance. This herd was left as a bait to the Crows should they come in quest of plunder.

When all these arrangements had been perfected, the warriors, numbering about forty, moved a little further up the Little Missouri in the direction in which the Crows would approach in order that they might have fresh grass for their ponies in close proximity to their lodges. The other parties started upon the hunt taking different lines but all in a general direction bearing south of east with the understanding that the rendezvous should be on the stream since known as the Cannon Ball River, about one hundred miles southeast of where they separated. Carefully did the Sioux warriors who were left behind to cover the hunters from a surprise from the Crows watch their herd of worthless ponies during the daytime when they knew it was possible they were being watched, but when night came they took good care to leave this same herd unprotected and of easy access, confining their watch to their own camp and their good horses that were always kept therein as soon as darkness approached.

Finally one morning about ten days after they had been left to guard, they were rewarded by finding the decoy herd gone. All indications went to prove that the Crows had taken them early in the night and had therefore gone a long distance with them before discovering their worthlessness.

After several days of waiting and watching the Sioux warriors began to move a short distance each day in the direction of the hunting party, which they overtook in the course of time, and dividing joined their respective family groups and assisted in the prosecution of the hunt until it was finished and the village had again established itself, this time upon the Cannon Ball River, as previously arranged.

After they had fully decided to remain on the Cannon Ball River for the winter, couriers were dispatched to guide in the traders. While these were gone and the women were busily engaged in tanning robes, a spirit of adventure seized many of the young men afresh, and they decided to have another tilt with their enemies. There-

fore, two war parties were organized, one consisting of
fifteen with Red Cloud as its leader and one of twelve
with Young Man Afraid of His Horse as its leader. The
first was to go against the Crows and the second against
the Snakes.

Red Cloud and his party left the village two days before the other and traveling west and north reached a
branch of the Little Missouri a little after dark on the
second day. Selecting a small opening in the thick timber
and brush they unpacked their horses. As it was late and
quite dark, they decided not to build any fire as they now
considered themselves very close to the enemy's country. After taking their horses to the edge of the wood and
picketing them, they retired for the night. Next morning
they were surprised to find their horses gone. After a little
investigation they found where there had been another
party camped below them on the river. Every indication
pointed to the fact that the party was composed of Crows
who had been en route to the Sioux village. The two
opposing war parties had met at this point unknown to
each other, and the Crows had reaped a benefit by discovering the fact first. As a consequence Red Cloud and
his party were afoot and were compelled to walk home.

In about ten days after the return to their village and
before their friends had ceased to chaff them about their
adventure, Young Man Afraid of His Horse and party
returned from their trip to the Snakes. They had met
with better success, bringing nearly a hundred head of
fine horses and quite a number of buffalo robes, having
put a small Snake village to rout.[3]

14

Escape by Boat

IF RED CLOUD COULD BE remembered for only one exploit, the following would be a leading candidate. Trapped by enemy Rees, Red Cloud depended upon his wits to escape and his will to survive.

The Ree, or Arikara, tribe, who dwelled along the Missouri River for generations, had suffered greatly from the ravages of disease and from clashes with the Lakotas and other nomadic enemies. By the 1850s remnants of the tribe were confined to a single earthlodge village in present North Dakota.[1]

Disparagingly termed "river Indians" by Red Cloud, the Arikaras needed conveyances to cross the Missouri and resorted to the "bull hide boat," a curious invention.[2] It consisted of buffalo hides stretched tightly over a round framework of willow, not the most seaworthy of watercraft and definitely not the equivalent of an Eastern Woodlands dugout canoe, which the Arikaras did not build. Although the word "canoe" is used throughout this story, that may be a translator's error; the Lakota words for "canoe" and "boat" are quite similar.[3] Knowing that Red Cloud paddled to freedom in an unwieldy tub of fur, not its sleek wooden counterpart, makes his feat all the more amazing.

The village remained on the Cannon Ball River during the following winter, and, as only two small trading outfits reached them, whose goods were soon disposed of, the Indians fared badly. Having to rely entirely on their meager supply of dried meat for food, they soon ran short and had eaten most all of their dogs and were beginning to eat their horses to keep from starving until spring opened when they could go out in search of game. When the grass became strong enough to impart strength to their ponies, they moved north and camped among the numerous small tributaries of a considerable sized creek—since known as Heart Creek—that puts into the Missouri at old Fort Abraham Lincoln. In this locality where game was abundant they recuperated and fattened their horses and spent the summer of 1857.

About the middle of the summer, however, camp life grew too monotonous for the active men in the village, and several war parties were organized for the purpose of raiding their enemies. Two parties went west to attack the Crows and Snakes, while Red Cloud with twenty-four others went north to fight the Ree Indians, who with several other tribes, including the Gros Ventres, Piegans, Bloods, and Blackfeet, had their habitation on the Upper Missouri, ranging from where Fort Berthold Reservation is now located north and west on the Milk River and other tributaries of the Missouri.

Red Cloud and his party had traveled about one hundred and fifty miles when they came to the Missouri River. After reconnoitering for a while they discovered a small cluster of lodges located in the edge of the timber near the river. They knew by the style of their lodges that they were not Rees. Their horses were feeding along the outer edge of the river bottom and along the hills, and the Sioux looked upon them already as their own. But they had traveled a long distance, and it had been many moons since they had done any fighting. They were anxious to engage in battle with the river Indians, whom they held in contempt for preferring the lowlands of the river and the mosquitoes to the breezy highlands and buffalo of the plains.

Managing to wind about through the hills and gullies until quite near to the village they were enabled to count the lodges. They figured that there were anywhere from thirty-five to forty fighting men in the party. With only these odds to contend against they calculated that it would be overcome by surprising them, and they could easily put them to rout.

As soon as this point was decided upon, they charged. It was a little after noon, and they went toward the village on a run, yelling like so many fiends, with their eagle feathers and war trappings flying in the breeze.

The party attacked proved to be Gros Ventres, and they were completely surprised, but they decided not to be routed.[4] On the contrary they rallied between the Sioux and their lodges and effectually repulsed them. After an exchange or two of volleys of arrows and bullets, the Sioux veering to the north ran off a little way and, seeing that they were not followed, stopped and counciled for a few minutes, then came back as before on a full run.

The Gros Ventres, who had stood their ground awaiting their return, received them with a well directed volley that brought one of their number to the ground dead and wounded three others. The man killed was hurriedly gathered up by two of his comrades, and the Sioux wheeling to the west retreated again. Again the Gros Ventres improved the opportunity to reload, but the Sioux after another council scattered out and rounded up over a hundred head of horses and moved off over the hills in the direction from which they came. The Gros Ventres made no pretense of following them, but seemed to be satisfied in having successfully defended their homes without trying to recover their horses.

The Sioux seeing they were not pursued continued to travel west among the hills until dark. Then they changed their course and followed down a small creek that led to the south. They traveled long enough to lose themselves to anyone who might have been watching them and then went into camp and buried the one of their number who had been killed in the branches of a large elm tree. The wounds of the others were examined and washed and found not to be so severe as to prevent traveling. Then a consultation was engaged in while they were eating their supper of dried meat, which resulted in ten of them, including those who were wounded, going on with the herd to their own village, while Red Cloud and thirteen others remained where they were until daylight.

Then they went in a southeasterly direction toward the river in search of the Rees, the Indians that they had come out particularly to encounter. They traveled very slowly and kept under cover of brush and hills all the time. Along towards the middle of the afternoon they gained a point from which they could see the Ree village several miles down the river situated between the point of [the] bluff that put in from the west and the river bank on the east. As they had anticipated, the village was large, for the Rees had learned by bitter experience to keep together for protection against their old enemies, the Sioux.

They were strictly river Indians and always had their home along the edge of the water, either of the Missouri or some of its tributaries. Their houses were built of sticks and saplings pla[i]ted and woven together and daubed with mud inside and out, making when complete a sort of adobe. Some of them were built round and others oval shaped and had roofs that were rounded in to the center where an opening was left that answered the double purpose of chimney and window. The houses were generally built in pairs closely adjoining each other with a door or small opening between. One of these rooms was used for a stable in which their horses were placed nights. Their villages being composed of such structures were necessarily more permanent than those of the plains Indians. While these river Indians owned a great many horses, they were not entirely dependent upon them as a means of transportation, for they were all experts with the canoe, large numbers of which were always to be found moored along the bank of the river near their village.

The Sioux from their hiding place watched the Ree village, which was all astir but showed no evidence of excitement. As the shadows of night commenced to fall, Red Cloud and his party began to move cautiously through the breaks and gullies getting nearer and nearer to the village. The Rees had rounded up their horses in the early part of the evening, and they were standing quietly at the edge of the village, having become accustomed to being corralled nights.

The Sioux had decided to make a rush and stampede the herd and, if an opportunity presented itself, shoot a straggling Ree or two and escape with their booty. For this purpose they waited until it was quite dark. Then crouching low upon their horses they advanced part way across the bottom that separated them from the herd, then made a charge.

When within an arrowshot of the horses there arose a line of Rees from the earth on each side that immediately closed in behind them and gave them a volley of bullets and arrows that knocked two of them from their horses. The Rees had been notified by the Gros Ventres of the presence of the Sioux and had ambushed them.

Red Cloud and one other was in the lead of the party, and their horses carried them along among the Ree horses before they could check them. As soon as they could, however, they dismounted and sought refuge among the loose horses which were being held in front by a row of horses and on the sides by Rees who were left to guard them and in the rear by the combatants.

Red Cloud and his partner managed to keep between the frightened horses, but, as they were shifting about and breaking away in small bunches, this was a difficult job. Presently a few that had become more excited than the rest started upon a keen gallop to break away. The Indian that was with Red Cloud seized one of these by the tail with both hands and went with the flying horses. In the meantime the fight was still raging although it had shifted further back toward the bluffs, and there were Rees moving about between the herd and the fight. Red Cloud realized that it was time to act if he wished to escape. He was pretty sure the Rees did not know that he was among the horses. If they did, they would not be firing into their own herd to get him, but this protection was only temporary. Something must be done and that quickly.

He hit upon the following plan and proceeded to execute it at once. Dodging along among the horses he drew his blanket over his head and face. Wrapping it closely about him with his gun concealed beneath he stepped boldly out into the Ree village and began walking toward the river. It was quite dark, but the lights shone from the tops of the lower buildings. While most of the inhabitants were congregated a little way out on the river bottom in the direction of the fight, there were still some moving about the village. He was passed once or twice but not accosted. There being nothing in his appearance to attract particular attention—he being nothing but an Indian walking through an Indian village—he soon got near enough to the river so as to feel that if necessary he could run and make his escape certain. But he was resolved not to run unless discovered.

He had reached the incline that led to the bank of the river and was beginning to increase his walk a trifle when he met a woman and a little girl who had been down after water. As they passed, the woman said something to him that he did not understand, but he replied with a sort of grunt and kept on his way, and the woman went over to the village with the water.

Red Cloud's only object had been to reach the river. Once there he felt that he could plunge in and swim to safety, but, when he descended the bank, he saw several canoes. Cutting one of them loose he got into it. He knew very little about managing the thing, but after a few awkward strokes he succeeded in getting out into the channel when it began to ride away from the Ree village. This was what he most desired. By using only one paddle he succeeded in crowding his canoe out further and further into the main channel, which gradually shifted to the opposite bank carrying Red Cloud and the boat with it.

All firing had now ceased at the village, and soon he saw the Rees with torches approach the river, but this was but a natural thing for them to do after the fight as they evidently put a value upon their canoes nearly if not quite equal to that of their horses. They were no doubt just looking over them in a general way to see if they had been disturbed and did not miss the one Red Cloud took. At any rate they did not follow him, and he drifted along down the swift current all that night.

He found some difficulty in keeping the canoe from brushing the banks at times, but beyond this his course down the river during the night of his escape was without incident. He thought several times that he would make a landing upon the west bank and strike through the country on foot, but he concluded that most of his companions had been killed and such as had made their escape were scattered among the hills and would in all probability be pursued by the Rees and that it would be safest to keep to the river until he had been carried beyond their reach.

The next morning shortly after daylight he began to experience a sense of hunger and kept close watch for any kind of game that might be seen along the river banks. But several hours passed away, and he was unable to discover anything that would afford him meat. Finally feeling unable to suffer longer he guided the canoe into a small creek that he saw putting into the river. Getting out he pulled it up the stream a short distance and made it fast. Then taking his gun he started up the creek. Raising an eminence that afforded him a good view of the surrounding country, he took a good look but could see nothing in the shape of game or humanity. Continuing his walk across a little valley he scared up a flock of prairie chickens which lighted in the trees near the creek. Taking careful aim at one he shot and killed it. He ran and picked it up greedily, and tearing the feathers off he took out his butcher knife and removed the entrails. Then stepping to the creek he washed it, and cutting it into pieces of convenient size, he devoured it raw. After the bones had been thoroughly picked, he wrapped himself in his blanket and crawling into the brush laid down and took a much needed sleep.

It was nearly sundown when he awoke, much refreshed. Getting his canoe he pushed it out into the river and again started on his journey. He traveled nights without any interruption, but during the day he would stop to hunt and sleep and get views of the country to see if the coast was clear and consequently made very little distance during the day.

During the first part of the fourth night as he was moving along rapidly in the main current, he heard a faint sound that seemed to come from down the river. Listening attentively it grew more distinct as he advanced. In a little while he could distinguish the barking of dogs and the beating of drums and knew that he was nearing an Indian village, which he hoped would prove to be some band of the Missouri River Sioux. After a time he came in sight of lights. Then he began to keep his canoe in the shadow of the river bank as much as possible. When he had come sufficiently near, he stopped, tied his canoe to some shrubbery, and advanced through the wood to the edge of the village and paused to listen. Presently he heard an old Indian haranguing in his own language. He stepped boldly into the opening and advanced to the village and found that he was among his friends, a band of Brule Sioux who were delighted when they learned that they had the great Red Cloud as their guest and were very much interested in the story of the fight and the escape.[5]

After resting here for several days during which time he was feasted and counciled continually, the Brules made him a present of several fine horses and furnished him with provisions and two young men as companions. He left their village for his own under circumstances so favorable that he arrived at home on the fifth day. There was great rejoicing when he entered the village, for it was supposed that he had been killed.

After his arrival he learned the fate of his comrades. The ten who had come in with the Gros Ventres horses had arrived all right, and the horses were properly divided, Red Cloud's family getting his share. But of the fourteen who went to the Ree village, Red Cloud made the seventh who had come back. Two others arrived the day after he got home, one of whom died a short time after his arrival from wounds received in the fight, and five, among whom was the man who tried to break through the cordon by holding to the horse's tail, were never heard from.

15

Revenge

THE FOLLOWING STORY of a brutal attack by Red Cloud's Oglalas on a passing village of Arapahos, members of a tribe with close ties to the Lakotas, may seem unlikely. Yet credence should be given it. The Sioux were traditional enemies of the "Gros Ventres of the Prairie" or Atsina tribe, kinsmen to the Arapahos, and two clues in the historical record suggest that precedents existed for occasional flare-ups between the Lakotas and Arapahos.

In 1930 He Dog, a nephew of Red Cloud, recalled that his friend Crazy Horse had battled some Arapahos when both were about eighteen years old (Crazy Horse was born about 1840). The Arapahos fought from "a high hill covered with big rocks and near a river." Crazy Horse took two scalps.[1]

The other source is a pencil drawing credited to geologist Ferdinand V. Hayden, now in the New York State Library in Albany. Hayden explored the Dakotas beginning in 1853, and sometime in the decade he drew and labeled "Scalp Mountain and Scenery in Cretaceous Formation—Sioux exterminated a village of Rappahoes on this Mountain." Although the chronology and geography are difficult to reconcile, this may be the site of the story that follows.[2]

⫯

Red Cloud and his people spent the fall in hunting. They were favorably located, being far removed from their enemies, and, as the other parties that had gone to the Snakes and Crows had met with strong resistance and had returned considerably worsted, with a loss of seven men, they concluded to discontinue their raids and act entirely on the defensive for a time. After shifting their camp to a desirable location, a few days east and south of their summer home, they spent the winter in practicing their native sports and in idleness.

In the early part of the summer of 1858 they decided to move south again and consequently began to drift back towards the Black Hills. When they reached the head of Grand River, they went into camp near the base of Eagle Nest Mountain and remained there for some time. One morning the news was brought to camp that an Indian village was seen moving to the northeast, coming from the direction of Slim Buttes, which lay about twenty-five miles to the southeast of their camp.

Preparations were hurriedly made, and in a very short time two or three hundred warriors were mounted and en route for the moving village. It was a damp, foggy

day. As they were traveling through a rough, broken country, they were unable to see any considerable distance
and consequently had forerunners ahead to report to
them from time to time on the progress and direction of
the movers and to guide them to a point where they might
intercept them with the most advantage.

It was in the early part of the afternoon when their
scouts, from an eminence a little in advance, signaled them
to halt, which they did. Presently they saw the caravan of
travois winding slowly around the side of a hill at right
angles with them. The Sioux were uncertain what tribe
the village belonged to but surmised that they were either Cheyennes or Arapahos, and with either of these
tribes they were not at war. They decided that if they
were Cheyennes they would not molest them, but on
the contrary if they were Arapahos they would give them
battle for the reason that the Arapahos and Gros Ventres
were branches of the same tribe. The Sioux were still sting-
ing under the defeat and loss they had sustained on the
Upper Missouri at the hands of the Gros Ventres and by
the Rees, who had been warned of the presence of the
Sioux by the former named tribe.

Consequently, it was with a great deal of interest that
they watched the approaching column that was traveling
slowly and in regular aboriginal style with the old man,
the head of the family, in the lead astride his pony with a
red bandage about his forehead, his reins in one hand
and his whip in the other, and his gun and bow and quiver
upon his back. Behind him came his squaw or squaws,
and about them the younger members of the family, all
mounted, also one, two, or three sleepy old ponies that

were harnessed to the travois made of the poles of their lodges, on which were placed their household goods and baskets formed in wickets or cages, some of which contained papooses and others puppies that were too young to travel. Some young men were prancing about on their war horses, either singly or in groups, while others were engaged in the more laborious task of driving the loose horses.

All this formed a picture that would at once rivet and hold the attention of one unaccustomed to such scenes, and it also engaged the close attention of the Sioux, but for reasons far different from anything approaching a love of the romantic. When the moving village had wound around the hillside and had reached a small plateau, the Sioux knew that there were fifty families and that they were not expecting to be molested. They were therefore not surprised at the consternation that seized the travelers when Red Cloud and a dozen others rode suddenly to the top of an adjacent hill and motioned for them to stop. The Sioux then asked them in the sign language who they were. They replied that they were Arapahos. On inquiry as to where they were going, they answered that they were going north to visit their relations, the Gros Ventres.

This sealed their doom, for while the party on the hill kept them in conversation for a time, using the sign language exclusively, the rest of the Sioux were gradually surrounding them. When the Arapahos noticed this movement, they began to bear off toward the only opening that seemed left for escape. But no sooner did the Sioux see that their game had taken the scent than they made a charge. They were met on the strongest side by the

Arapahos and driven back for a moment, but instantly the Arapahos found themselves attacked on the other side and presently from all sides. They were so outnumbered as to be unable either to escape or resist, and the Sioux killed them all, except the women and children, many of whom were also killed or mortally wounded during the fray. But such as were not were taken to the Sioux village, where many of them remained, while others joined their people further south when an opportunity presented itself.

This was the Sioux revenge for their mishap among the Rees and Gros Ventres. The fact that it fell on innocent victims made no difference to them so long as the victims were related to the hated tribes.

16

The Snake Fort

RED CLOUD'S EPIC ADVENTURES continued with another encounter with Shoshone, or Snake, warriors, although this war expedition displayed a different form and function. Instead of merely searching for plunder, Red Cloud and his followers methodically searched for intruders to expel from Lakota lands.

Battles on the plains assumed unique characteristics that reflected the region's open lands and flat terrain. The specific feature illustrated in this story is an outnumbered opponent's mad dash for the refuge of high ground, itself a rare commodity on occasion. For the Snakes chased by Red Cloud the relative safety of their stone haven proved short-lived.

Sometimes the tales of long ago defensive struggles at these natural forts provided a site's modern name. A pursuing Sioux party chased Crow raiders to Crow Butte, a northwestern Nebraska landmark, for example, and forced them to climb to its summit for safety. The Crow

Butte incident, which occurred in 1849, is extensively documented and boasts a historical marker. By contrast, the location of the encounter described here is unknown today.[1]

Also noteworthy in this story is an instance of Red Cloud's marksmanship. When trader Francis Salway first met Red Cloud in the 1850s, the latter "was shooting at a mark with a gun." A half century later, Salway recalled Red Cloud being "a good shot, one of the best shots I have seen among the Indians."[2]

⁓

The Oglalas after their annihilation of the Arapaho village kept on moving south until they reached Fort Laramie late in the fall. They had finished their fall hunt and went into camp for the winter. They were abundantly supplied with robes, and traders in the vicinity of the fort were numerous. They remained near the old post and enjoyed the accommodations that were obtainable from the prairie merchants until late in the following summer, at which time their annual hunt necessitated a move. They drifted north and west again, making their hunt on the Powder River country. Later in the fall they located their winter camp on the headwaters of the Belle Fourche on the west side of the Black Hills. When they became settled in their camp, couriers were sent to Fort Laramie to guide traders to it. About twenty days after their departure they returned to the village with four traders who had several wagons each, and all were heavily loaded with goods.

During the absence of these couriers Red Cloud left the village with seventy-five warriors for the purpose of scouting the country to the west and driving out their old enemies, either Snakes or Crows, that he might find and thereby protect the village from interruption during the winter. The party had moved very leisurely, sometimes scattering out and covering several different sections of the country at the same time. Then meeting again at a chosen point they would travel in a body.

They had continued their march in this manner for about ten days and had looked through the country pretty thoroughly as far as the Big Horn Mountains and were reconnoitering through this range when they espied a large party of Indians. A little observation disclosed the fact that it was a war party headed in the direction of the Sioux country and that it was composed of about fifty men. They soon discovered also that the party had discovered them.

Then came a series of maneuvers from each side that resulted in the Sioux making the first advance, the other part[y] veering from the small stream up which they had been traveling to the north in the direction of a low spur of rocky hills that extended out from the mountains. They were nearly all on foot, having but a few horses with which to scout and carry provisions. When the Sioux, who were all mounted, came to their trail along the creek, they discovered by their moccasin tracks that they were Snakes.

The country was rough, and the Sioux could get no opportunity to charge but kept following as best they could and firing whenever a good chance presented itself. The Snakes, who seemed to know just where they

were going and what they were going there for, kept
steadily making for the rocky point toward which they had
first started. The Sioux leaving their horses hitched in the
brush that skirted the creek, started after them on foot
and pressed them so closely that one of their number was
killed and one Sioux disabled by a piece of rock hitting
him in the face that had been shattered by a musket ball.

Finally the Snakes reached the goal for which they
had been running and climbing. They almost immediately disappeared behind the walls of rock that with the
exception of an opening here and there formed a natural
fort. Picking the loose rock that everywhere abounded
both inside and outside the fort they began to pile them
up, filling up the gaps, and they were soon well fortified.
The Sioux by this time had surrounded the point upon
which they were entrenched and taking shelter behind
huge boulders themselves were harassing the Snakes
whenever an opening or low place in the walls or uneven
ground would afford an opportunity. As the Sioux would
run from rock to rock, the Snakes would fire upon them
and while thus exposed would be fired upon in turn by
others of the Sioux who were under cover.

In this manner the fight continued for some time
when the Snakes, fearing a continuous siege and being
without water and food, began to evidence a disposition
to extricate themselves by becoming more determined in
their defense. Frequently they would jump upon the wall
to get a crack shot at one of the Sioux, and in this way
several Sioux were wounded. Red Cloud, noting the point
where one brave Snake was exposing himself at intervals,
carefully crawled from one rock to another until he was

in the right position. When the Snake again showed himself upon the wall, he took deliberate aim and firing instantly killed him. He fell to the outside of the wall.

The Snake had scarcely struck the ground before Red Cloud, rushing forward with raised tomahawk, sprang upon his prostrate body. He was now protected by the wall himself as the Snakes could not harm or even see him without exposing themselves. As all the interest of the Sioux now centered upon this point, he was amply covered and protected by the guns of others of his party. Red Cloud seeing that the Snake was dead, he chopped off one of his arms at the shoulder and scalped him, then holding the dismembered arm upon the wall shouted for them to come out and fight if they were brave.

While this scene was being enacted, so much interest was manifested by the Sioux in what was transpiring at that particular side of the fortification that they began to rush to that point leaving the other side unguarded. The Snakes took advantage of this and leaping over the wall broke through the few scattering guards that were left in the direction which they ran, killing one of them as they passed. The Snakes took a downhill run towards the Sioux horses, but, seeing the Sioux start in a body after them, they changed their course and scattered among the mountains where it was impracticable for their pursuers to follow. The Sioux, gathering up their wounded and killed, started back for the plain to the east but not before they examined the Snake fort and found therein one dead and two wounded, which latter they quickly dispatched.

It was nearly dark when they left the high and gloomy mountains behind them and filed across a broad plain until they came to a small stream running east. This they followed down for some distance and finally stopped and buried their dead comrade. Then continuing on for some distance under the cover of darkness they finally camped for the night.

From this camp they spent several days in riding north and south along the foot of the range in order to show such of their enemies as might be watching from the mountains that they were determined to dispute any encroachment that might be made upon their territory. When they finally concluded that they had sufficiently patrolled their frontier to insure them from attack for a long time, they withdrew during the night in order that their whereabouts might remain a secret to their enemies as long as possible and returned to their own village at the foot of the Black Hills.

17

Traders

THE OGLALA "SOLDIERS," or *akicita*, appear again in this
story, but roles are reversed from the earlier episode, and
Red Cloud is nearly on the receiving end. Sam Deon,
who now figures prominently in the narrative, deflects
the wrath of the Lakota *akicita* through quick thinking.
With Deon's appearance—he told Addison E.
Sheldon in 1902 that he first came to Red Cloud's camp
in the winter of 1860—the autobiography undergoes
conspicuous changes and takes on a different character.[1]
No longer merely the intermediary between Red Cloud
and Charles Allen, Deon now serves as an additional witness to the events recounted. More dialogue and additional details are included, and more names of minor
characters are listed, such as Deon's employer Geminien
P. Beauvais and Fort Laramie trader William Houston.
And the result? Red Cloud shares center stage in the
narrative's remaining pages with the little Frenchman
from Montreal.

During Red Cloud's absence from camp a strange scene was enacted there. The four traders, who had pitched their camp in different parts of the village, had begun their traffic. Their goods consisted of dry goods and groceries and Indian trinkets suitable to the trade. As they were all what were called legitimate traders and the Indians were well stocked with robes, skins, and other tradable goods, prospects seemed fair for a good trade.

One of the traders was a man by the name of Samuel Deon, a small, dark complexioned, smart, wiry, little Frenchman from Montreal, Canada. He could speak the Sioux language fluently and was a great friend of Red Cloud, whose lodge he always made his headquarters when upon trading expeditions, which he had been making to Fort Laramie for several years in the interest of Beauvais & Co. of St. Louis, Missouri. On this occasion, as usual, he had placed his four large Murphy wagons immediately in the rear of Red Cloud's lodge and had taken out a number of goods and placed them within the lodge and had begun his trade.[2] He had four hired men who had driven the teams and who were now engaged in herding the cattle and in getting up wood for the winter's fire. For these he had constructed a tipi near the wagons in which they cooked and ate and slept.

On their trip to the village Deon's men had been in the habit of putting out strychnine at their camp for the purpose of poisoning wolves. Knowing this and being thoroughly versed in the customs and affairs of Indian life, Deon warned his men not to place any more poison, for it would be sure to cause the death of some of the Indian dogs and thereby create trouble.[3] With this and other precautions Deon established himself in a manner that he felt would allow him to devote his whole mind and time to the trade, which was now moving smoothly.

The flaunting of bright, new, blue cloth blankets by the men and the display of many colored blankets and red, green, and yellow calico by the women showed that the inhabitants of the village were fast discarding their old robes for the new costumes brought by the traders. Women too were everywhere seen roasting and boiling coffee until the air was laden with the exhilarating aroma of that famous bean and feasting with boiled side [meat?] and hominy and other edibles both purchased and native for their menu.

All seemed joy, contentment, and peace, when one day in the middle of the forenoon Red Cloud's wife came to Deon and told him that the Indian soldiers were going to give the traders a severe chastisement. Deon inquired the reason and was informed that his men had placed some poison where it had killed ten good dogs. Some young men who had gone after horses in the morning had found them and had skinned them and sold the hides to the other traders. They would be soldiered upon for buying the hides, and he would be dealt with in like manner because his men put out the poison.

The woman was much excited during the recital of the information for it meant the destruction of her own lodge, wherein Deon had his goods. Deon inquired of his men if they had put out strychnine. Yes, they had poisoned the carcass of a dead horse that lay in the vicinity of where they herded cattle. Deon informed them that it would probably cost them dearly and gave them a slight idea of what it meant to have his goods and lodge soldiered upon. Presently he saw the soldiers move out from where the large soldier lodge stood. They were about fifty in number and all mounted and were moving in double fire [file].

The soldiers, as they were called, are the supreme rulers of the village. Their actions are usually determined by the council, over which of course the chief exercises a great influence, but nothing approaching absolute authority, for a chief depends upon his popularity for his authority, which enables him to bring a great number of fighting men to his support upon occasions of importance. In order to maintain this control he must keep in line with the popular customs and usages of his people. Therefore, a chief is in many respects amenable to the law of the soldiers inasmuch that, if he should openly defy the execution of an edict once agreed upon, they would force him to acquiesce in precisely the same manner that they would the poorest Indian of the tribe. The action of the Indian soldier, therefore, while barbarous and terrible, is impartial, and they are feared, obeyed, and when in action shunned by everyone. Their intention is not to kill but to terrify and sometimes to whip the offenders and in every instance to destroy everything they touch belonging to them. For this purpose they provide themselves with long sticks, whips, small axes, and sometimes old swords, all weapons of distinction, and [a] few are provided with pistols which they only fire in the air as a warning that they are coming at which time it is expected that everyone will get out of their way; they almost always do. The soldiers moved to one of the trader's lodges on the opposite side of the village. The trader's name was William Huston [Houston], an American and a new hand at the business, who could not speak or understand the Sioux language. Not having any idea what was the matter he failed to run away from his goods until several shots had been fired by the approaching party, one or two of which struck among his wagons and broke a spoke out of a wheel just as he was leaving, almost being pulled away by his Indian friends who had some difficulty in making him understand what he ought to do. As the soldiers came to the lodge, they began to ride around it in a circle, striking it, and cutting and chopping until it fell to the ground a ruined mass. This done they went to the lodge of a trader by the name of Fuson. There they repeated the operation, then doing the same thing to the lodge of the other trader, one Moran [Edward D. Morin]. They turned in the direction of Deon's wagons and Red Cloud's lodge.

Deon had been watching them and had almost given up in despair at the foolish inconvenience and losses to which he was about to be subjected, when, being a man of quick wit and action and understanding the Indian disposition thoroughly, he resolved to try a ruse that had for its base an appeal not to the hearts of the approaching mob but to their stomach. Summoning Red Cloud's wife and stopping an old woman who was hurrying by, he told them to go with him and meet the soldiers. They hesitated at first, for they considered it a bold undertaking, but he insisted and told them that he would stay right behind them. He charged them particularly to stay right in the path and force the Indians to ride around them, informing them that they dared not run over them but on the contrary would ride around them if they would only be firm. He instructed them to sing out as loud as possible, when they came to the foremost, to spare her lodge and she would give them a tea kettle feast and to keep on crying this until all of them had passed.

With this understanding the trio started, the two women in front and Deon close behind them. As they approached the Indians, Deon encouraged them to be firm and not get out of the way but force the soldiers to do so. This they did.

Red Cloud's wife holding up her hands began crying, "Oh, my friends, take pity on me, and do not look back at my lodge, and I will give you a feast. Pass it by, and do not see it, and I will fill you up with a great feast." And this she kept repeating until they had all passed.

When the soldiers came to her lodge, they rallied about the little temporary tipi that Deon had for a cook house and after demolishing it went on their way. Red Cloud's lodge was not molested nor Deon's goods further than some of his cooking utensils were destroyed. After this cloud had passed over, affairs of the village resumed their usual serenity. The discomfited traders soon had their trading posts repaired, and everything was going as though nothing had occurred.

But Deon was more than pleased at the speedy return of his old friend, Red Cloud, who was also pleased to find that Deon had been the means of saving his lodge from the wrath of the soldiers.[4] As he and Deon were great friends, they had an enjoyable time, Red Cloud telling his experiences on the chase and Deon in raking in the sheckels in the forms of robes and pelts until the opening of spring. Then he left them and returned to Fort Laramie.

The village moved around to the east side of the Black Hills where the summer was spent in hunting and visiting other Sioux tribes along the tributaries of the Missouri River. On the headwaters of Medicine Creek that empties into the Missouri a short distance above where Fort Thompson was afterward located, the Oglalas spent the winter. Drifting back to the North Platte during the summer of 1861, they went into winter camp about sixty miles above Fort Laramie. From this camp Red Cloud sent word to Deon to come and make the winter trade with them.

Upon this occasion Red Cloud had a large lodge erected near his own. When Deon came, he had him corral his wagons around it and place his goods inside. Then a great feast was given to all the leading men, and the price and the rules of the trade were agreed upon. Then the exchange of goods began and went smoothly on until one day about mid-winter. When Deon was in the lodge alone, a woman entered and asked that she be given a piece of blue cloth for nothing. Deon, accustomed to being begged of and not noticing anything peculiar in the manner of the woman, refused her. She left the lodge, and shortly afterwards there was a great howling and crying among the women in some adjacent lodges.

Presently Red Cloud's brother, Big Spider, entered

in a very sullen manner and going to the rear of the lodge picked up his gun and sat down and began cleaning it in a way that showed something of importance was on his mind. Deon had spoken to him as he entered the lodge and had received no reply. He now began watching his movements with curious interest. Big Spider sat there with his head hung, his hands hurriedly and nervously wiping out his gun. Deon knew that his heart was bad and that he was bent on mischief. Putting the facts of the woman entering and asking for cloth and the subsequent crying of the women and Big Spider's manner of entering the lodge together, he quickly concluded that there was a mistake somewhere and that Big Spider had been deceived and that he, Deon, was the intended victim. Having come to a full and correct understanding of the situation, he resolved on quick action. Like a flash he sprang to his feet immediately in front of Big Spider, and demanded in the Dakota [Lakota] language, "What is the matter with you? What do you mean?"

Startled by this sudden demonstration of nerve and agility, Big Spider looked up. As he did so, his eyes gazed into the muzzle of Deon's revolver. "Tell me quickly what is wrong and who has been lying to you!" said Deon.

The Indian, dropping his gun, replied, "You made my cousin cry by refusing to give her a piece of cloth to cover her dead child, and I came to kill you."

"You won't kill me today. You will be further off from me than you are now when you kill me, and what you say is a lie. I never refused to give a woman cloth to cover her child, and I never knew a child had died," responded Deon. Reaching down he picked up a piece of blue cloth and tearing off two or three yards handed it to him, saying, "There, take that to your cousin. I will not only furnish the cloth for a shroud, but if necessary I will go and wrap up the child myself. I am not a dog. I am a man."

Big Spider took the cloth with the customary acknowledgement of "How!" and departed, leaving his gun. At this juncture Red Cloud was heard approaching and crying in a loud voice, "Why did you want to harm my friend? You have always been wanting me to get a trader, and, when I got one and a good man, you want to kill him," and he rushed excitedly into the lodge from which Big Spider had just gone and was happily surprised to find his friend living and well.

Deon soon explained the whole circumstance to him, and Red Cloud, giving him a congratulatory shake of the hand, told him that he was in a distant part of the village when the news was brought to him that his brother, Big Spider, had killed the trader. He hurried home as fast as he could but expected to find him dead. He said the whole thing was a mistake, or he [Big Spider] would not have taken the cloth and left his gun. He assured Deon that it would be all right, and it was, for Big Spider came back in due course of time and apologized by saying that he had listened to the woman lying and crying and that it had made his heart bad, but it was all right. So they shook hands and were friends.

18

The Whiskey Peddler

GOVERNMENT OFFICIALS LONG TRIED to stem the flow of
contraband alcohol to the Plains tribes, but their efforts
were sometimes halfhearted and oftentimes in vain. Even
the larger trading companies occasionally assisted in prohibition efforts because their competitors, the small, independent traders beholden to no one, benefited more from
the whiskey trade than they did. But liquor was too profitable a commodity to keep out of Indian country for long.[1]

Itinerant traders, such as the man "Fuson" in the
previous story or "Leghan" in this one, may remain relatively anonymous to history, but their impact on Plains
culture was profound. Here is a sobering example of the
deadly effects of illicitly traded liquor on the tranquility
and well-being of Red Cloud's village.

Red Cloud referred to the white man's drink as *mini
wakan*, "the water that makes men crazy." Charles Jordan,
a close associate of the old man during his reservation years,
once wrote that he had never seen Red Cloud intoxi-
cated or under the influence of alcohol.[2]

Again there was a long interval uninterrupted by any exciting events, during which time the traders enjoyed profitable traffic. But one of the wild unusual happenings incident to Indian life that are always liable to occur when least expected upset the whole village again in the early spring. One day it was reported through camp that there was a wagon drawn by a span of mules approaching camp. This within itself was a strange occurrence, for the trading season was near the close, and, aside from the wagons belonging to the traders and those seen at the post and on the emigrant trail, a wagon was an uncommon spectacle. Therefore, all the people of the village were out watching the approach of this one, which finally arrived, entering at a point near to where Red Cloud and Deon were standing. At sight of the latter the driver stopped his team and passed the usual salutations.

Deon recognized him as a fellow by the name of Leghan, whom he had frequently seen about Fort Laramie, and knew him to be one of those wild, reckless characters that used to hang about in the vicinity of military posts in the early days of the old west, characters not very bad but by no means very good, having a general predilection to engage in hazardous enterprises, and the fact that such enterprises were contrary to established rules or even unlawful in the eyes of these [the?] gentry. Having fully placed the man in his mind, Deon was not surprised when he informed him that he was loaded with whiskey and that he intended to trade it to the Indians. Deon told him that he was sorry that he had come, that he might get through all right but that he was liable to have trouble, but he added, "Since you are here with it, I will take the first gallon jug myself."

After explaining the matter to Red Cloud, the latter ordered the man to go to the further side of the village and camp. This Leghan did and as might be expected did a thriving business with his illicit goods. Everything went pleasantly for a while, the majority of the Indians remaining sober, and the minority more or less drunk.

After all, human nature is human nature. Wherever whiskey is being drunk to excess, trouble is liable to occur. Usually a drunken Indian has as much control over himself as a drunken white man and is far less dangerous that a drunken desperado when everything goes right, but the trouble is that, when anything does occur, there is no law or other restraining influence to check them.

Leghan had been in the village about two weeks and had disposed of about half of his liquor and had quite a number of horses and mules in consequence thereof. The white traders were reasonably fair customers, and Red Cloud, through the courtesies of Deon, no doubt had his regular toddy but was never drunk. In fact, I doubt if anyone ever saw him under the influence of liquor, although he has had plenty of opportunities, being in his earlier days frequently associated with army officers and other gentlemen about military posts, among whom he was not barred from participating in refreshments on account of being an Indian.[3]

It was a pleasant afternoon about the middle of April,

and all the village was astir with unusual activity. The warm sunshine and the tender sprouting green grass and the slowly budding shrubbery along the creek and river bottoms lent a soft invigorating perfume to the air that foretold the rapidly approaching spring. Here and there on the tops of adjacent hills were Indians, standing erect with their blankets folded closely about them and singing in praise or lamentations over their fortunes, good or bad.

Scattered through the village in different localities small companies of young men were walking together and amusing themselves throwing arrows ahead of them a distance of about ten feet, a kind of game, the test being to see which one could throw his arrows nearest to some selected object and the winner taking all the arrows thrown. Urchins of ten and twelve summers were running about without their blankets, their long hair and breechclouts floating in the breeze and their shirt collars open to their breasts, in search of birds, with their bows and arrows poised in momentary expectation of their prey. Joyous bands of young girls were parading through the winding avenues formed by the irregular positions of the tall lodges, while older women were cooking and otherwise busying themselves with their various duties. Groups of old and middle-aged men were sitting here and there at different lodges, chattering and smoking, many of them no doubt feeling quite comfortable in consequence of a few drinks of Leghan's best, or worst, but none of them were hilarious or boisterous. One looking upon the tranquil picture that the whole village presented upon this pleasant afternoon would find it difficult to believe that in a very few moments it would be all changed into a scene of tragedy, pandemonium, and terror. But it was. And this is the way it happened.

Near the central part of the village by a tall lodge a young man was standing wrapped in his blanket in such a manner as to cover his head and the greater part of his face. Near him, sitting upon a small log that lay beside the lodge, was his mother, an old woman. She was chattering to the young man in a plaintive and expostulating manner. It was evident that both she and her son had been drinking, for, as an old gray-haired man came riding by, mounted upon an old pony, the old woman, after first burying her face in her hands and indulging in a little hysterical whine, pointed to the old man on horseback who had now ridden quite a distance past them. "My son, do you see that man riding there? Thirty years ago that man made me cry, and he made you and your brothers and sisters cry also, for he killed your father."

The young man turned and reaching in the lodge took out his gun and leveled it at the old man, fired, killing him instantly. As the old man rolled from his pony to the ground, screams of alarm went forth from those who witnessed the cruel deed, and immediately the village was up in arms. Terror seized the young culprit, and he started to run, dodging between the lodges to escape the flying bullets that were being fired at him. Across the flat he ran, being pursued like a mad dog, but by jumping first to one side and then the other, making steady aim impossible, he reached the hills. But as he began his ascent, his pursuers, some of whom were mounted, gained on him so closely that he was several times wounded.

Pushing on along the rugged, rocky hillside, he finally

reached a ledge of rock, the face of which stood about ten feet perpendicular on the side of the hills and the crown being covered with huge boulders and stunted pines. Here he made a stand and began to return the fire, which had the effect of checking the advance of the infuriated mob and making their fire more careful, cautious, and deadly. The Indians who were mounted, among whom was a brother of the fugitive, made a detour around the point of the hill and began an approach from the other side over the ridge. Leaving their horses at the base they were soon on the summit of the hill, approaching from tree to tree to where the young man was concealed. That he was mortally wounded was evident to those below by the fact that the blood of his wounds began to dripple over the face of the ledge of rock upon which he lay. His firing was also wild and uncertain and without any effect except to check the advance.

Presently the voice of his brother was heard from among the pines above, calling upon him to surrender and telling him they were bound to get him sooner or later. For a moment a deathlike stillness prevailed among the throng below, each one straining his ears to hear a reply from the doomed man. He made no reply, however, but presently he was seen to drag himself up close to the edge of the precipice upon which he had taken refuge. Sitting upright he gazed down upon the wild mob below with his blood-begrimed visage, having more the appearance of some horrid phantom than that of a human being. He sat almost motionless until several shots were fired at him. As none of them took effect, he slowly and with evident pain lowered his gun and, placing the muzzle to his head, fired and fell over the ledge.

During this episode the traders were told by their respective landlords to remain indoors. Red Cloud placed a guard over the entrance of his lodge. Deon sent a note to Leghan to fly, but this proved to be unnecessary, for at the very beginning of the trouble that worthy, realizing what the consequences of such an unexpected affair might be to him, took his gun and quietly stole down through the brush while all eyes were following the murderer in his precipitous flight. His landlord, being a worthless old Indian with two squaws and a lot of dogs and without any influence or ability to protect him in such a crisis, had improved the opportunity offered him and sought his own safety. The old Indian and his two squaws in the meantime hurriedly tore down their tipi and moved it and their effects to a distant part of the village, leaving Leghan's tent and wagon standing where they were. One of the old women, however, had a kindly feeling for Leghan and had found time during her hurry in the morning to watch the course Leghan had taken. She had seen him go down through the thick brush, which though dense was without foliage and therefore was not sufficient to protect him from view, unless he should lie down close to the ground. And it was fortunate for him that he did not.

Suddenly turning to the right he went up a deep gulch that ran back into the hills and at the head of which there was a cluster of tall cedars. Up between these he climbed. Their matted and interwoven evergreen boughs screened him perfectly from sight, yet gave him a commanding view of the village and all that transpired there. And now that his chance of escape rested entirely on the slender possibility of no one having seen him seek this refuge, anyone who had passed through great and perfectly apparent danger can readily realize what Leghan's feelings must have been during this trying ordeal. The first thought that comes to one under such circumstances is that he is doomed, that his time has come, and that he is sure to die. Of this fact he was so quickly and thoroughly convinced that he became, in a measure, reconciled to his fate. Then reason comes to his rescue and points out one or two chances by which he may live. Hope at once takes a footing upon these chances, and the reversal of feeling is so sudden that one revels as it were in the effort and expectancy of ultimate escape from the danger.

Leghan from his hiding place soon saw the great concourse of Indians turn from their position at the foot of the hill where the tragedy had ended and approach his tent. Instantly it was set on fire. Then the showers of bullets went whizzing through the kegs, spilling the liquor upon the ground and increasing the blaze. This brilliant spectacle lasted but a few moments. Leghan wished that it might have lasted longer, but, as his wagon had been run into the fire and entirely consumed, there was nothing further for them to destroy.

Then the crowd seemed to scatter, many of them going to their homes. Leghan watched this proceeding with intense interest, hoping that quiet would be restored, but he soon saw that the soldiers had gathered and were making a search for him. His old landlord was hunted up, and from one of his old women it was learned that he had taken his gun and gone down into the brush. This was all they learned from her. As they hesitated to follow an armed man into possible ambush, they gathered along the brow of the hill overlooking the creek and began firing into the brush. They kept this up until evening, and in some places the brush was fairly mowed to the ground. But as evening approached, they withdrew a few at a time, and comparative quiet was again restored. Just as soon as it was dark enough, the old woman who had watched Leghan took a small bag of dried meat, a blanket, and a rope and stole out by a circuitous route to where he was hidden. He had already come down from his perch. At a distance the old woman cautiously made herself known to him. After explaining, as well as possible, that his horses and mules had been confiscated, she gave him the articles she had brought and advised him to go and to catch a horse if he could without danger, but to keep going. This he did, leaving the village with vastly more experience than when he had entered it.

A full account of his escape and the various feelings that he underwent was given by Leghan himself two months later at Fort Laramie to his old acquaintance Deon, to whom we are indebted for the minutes of the tragedy.

19

The Lost Children

RED CLOUD STEPPED AWAY further from his narrative in recounting this mythic tale of "the lost children." For the narrator to intertwine the telling of one's deeds with one's tribal history and myths is a common feature of Native American autobiographies.[1]

Around a campfire an unidentified Oglala narrator offered to his rapt listeners an elaborate and entertaining explanation for the origin of the Western Sioux bands. What ensues is a story somewhat devoid of supernatural or spiritual elements yet fascinatingly rich in historical detail. More importantly, as scholar Raymond J. DeMallie has noted, such tales must be understood as "statements of social and cultural unity . . . and [we must] not dismiss them as poorly remembered history."[2]

Happily, an independent source exists for this origin tale. Caspar Collins, a young army officer from Ohio, wrote home from Laramie in 1865 and related a Sioux tale of "lost children" that he heard. The story, which Collins described as "the manner in which the Sioux be-

came divided into twelve tribes," is remarkably similar to
this one by Red Cloud. Because Collins died later that
year, and because his papers were not published until
1927, he and Charles Allen could not have had knowledge of or been influenced by one another's versions.[3]

In the spring of 1862 the village moved back to Fort Laramie
and remained encamped along the Laramie and Platte
rivers until early fall, when the council decided they would
move north again and make their fall hunt and locate
somewhere near the head of the Belle Fourche. Deon
started for their village later with five large wagons, each
drawn by six yoke of oxen and all heavily loaded with
goods. He reached the village before snow fell and found
them in their winter camp about twelve miles below the
head of the Belle Fourche. He stopped with Red Cloud,
as usual, and was soon informed there were two other
traders in the village. One man by the name of H[ank]
C. Clifford was established with Old Man Afraid of His
Horse, while Brave Bear had a large trader's outfit at his
lodge under the charge of Nick Janis, a man of marked
intelligence and fine physique well known among all the
Sioux not only as a trader in the employ of the American
Fur Company but also as an interpreter who generally
officiated for the government commissioners on their
various trips from Washington to council with the Sioux.[4]
As these three traders were old acquaintances and as
Clifford and Janis had already established prices, there

was nothing left for Deon to do but to give a feast by way of advertising his wares and begin trade.

The early part of the winter was somewhat severe, and the long nights were spent about lodge fires of either one or the other of the traders in feasting with the leading men of the tribe, who would recount their various experiences in war and on the chase, tell stories, some novel, some new, and often such as bore the marks of legendary lore and tradition. Janis himself was a good conversationalist and a great story teller. His lodge was a great visiting place for the other traders after the day's trade had been finished, when during the long winter nights they would tell stories themselves or listen to the Indians' tales.

Upon one of these occasions Janis asked a very old Indian to tell a story. The old man, after slowly lighting his pipe and taking a whiff or two passed it on to his left-hand neighbor, then began: Many winters ago when I was a little boy, I often heard my grandfather, who was then a very old man, say that he had heard his father tell how the old men of the village would talk of the time, long, long, ago, when the Sioux lived far away towards the east and were all in one large village and under one chief. They had enemies to the south and southwest of them who gave them great annoyance. It was necessary to keep detachments from their village posted on the outskirts of their territory in that direction to fight these enemies back. From time to time these guardsmen and their families were regularly relieved and would return to the village. The bands taking their places would begin fresh onslaughts upon their enemies, who were gradually driven further away, until the Sioux following them finally established themselves in the country they occupied and returned not to the present band. But their absence decreased the strength of their village very little as it was a powerful one and under the leadership of a great war chief by the name of The Yellow Horse.

On the west of the village was another strong tribe who called themselves "The Cut Fingers" but who were called by the Sioux then and since the Cheyennes.[5] The relation between these people and ours had been that of a watchful, suspicious peace which finally ended in a war, in which our people were the victors. Having put the Cheyennes to route they kept following them up. Every year they would fight them and drive them further west until finally they had driven them across the Missouri River.[6]

It was not a war of extermination. They would take prisoners back and forth, and they seemed to have been fighting each other only for the reason that they had no other enemies to fight. But when they crossed the Missouri River, they soon discovered that there were powerful tribes of Indians both to the north and west of them. The Sioux, following the advice of their chief, The Yellow Horse, decided to quit fighting the Cheyennes and to make allies of them if possible. Accordingly messengers were sent to the Cheyenne village, among whom were fifteen of the fifty or more Cheyennes that the Sioux had long held as prisoners.

After traveling four days they came to the Cheyenne village. The Sioux remaining at a distance, the Cheyenne prisoners went into the village and made known the object of their visit. They were received cordially. The Sioux were escorted in and feasted and entertained in a hospitable manner until the following day, when a council was held at which the Sioux stated that they had been sent by their chief, The Yellow Horse, to ask the Cheyennes to move their village to a certain point midway between the two villages where they would be met by the Sioux village for the purpose of holding a great council that would have for its object the establishment of peace between the two tribes. The Cheyennes accepted the proposition and sent an escort of Sioux prisoners back with the messengers as an earnest indication of their intentions.

At the appointed time and designated place the tribes met and set up their villages close to each other. The next day the great council lodge of the Sioux having been chosen as the place to deliberate, the council began with the Sioux chief, The Yellow Horse, and the Cheyenne chief, Long Bow, as the leading spirits. The first half of the day was spent in making speeches, The Yellow Horse telling the Cheyennes that they had been fighting so long that they had become well acquainted and that they were neighbors and that during their wars each side had taken so many prisoners that they were now not only neighbors but relations and that they were in a new country where their rights were liable to be disputed by powerful tribes and it would be better for them to remain near to each other and to fight together in the future. He was followed by Chief Long Bow and others, all of whom favored the idea, and it was soon decided that such arrangements should be effected. The sun was now in the middle of the sky, and the council adjourned for the feast. The council met again after they had feasted and began to arrange the considerations of peace, deciding the boundaries of their respective territory and the signals by which they were to communicate in the event that either village should be attacked by an enemy.

During their discussion of these matters they were continually being disturbed by the boys and girls of the Sioux village, who in their wild and boisterous sports made such a din that the councillors could not hear each other speak. Several times The Yellow Horse sent his head soldier to order them to a more distant part of the village to play, but they would soon return. Finally becoming exasperated, The Yellow Horse called out the Indian soldiers and instructed them to take all the children between the ages of eight and fourteen and mount them on old ponies and instruct their relatives to furnish enough old lodges and old women to manage them and take them a short distance over a high ridge to another small creek and keep them there until the great council should be ended. He then explained the matter to the Cheyennes and adjourned again to meet in the evening.

After his order as to the children had been carried out, shortly after the lodge fires had been lighted that evening and the councillors who had assembled were engaged in the further discussion of their affairs, a yell was heard a little distance from the council lodge. Immediately the council broke up in a stampede, some rushing for the entrance, others drawing their knives and slashing them through the lodge, making this their way of exit. It was dark, but someone was heard to hollow [holler?] in the Cheyenne tongue, "I am killed," and another was loudly boasting in the Sioux tongue, "I killed him."

It was afterwards found that a Cheyenne had stolen a Sioux's wife and had been discovered by the injured Sioux and shot, but it was not investigated at that time, for panic seized the people of both villages.[7] With the rapidity of magic their lodges were torn down and packed. Each village started at breakneck speed in opposite directions, running from each other. On they went in their wild confusion, each band imagining that the other was pursuing them.

When they had traveled half the night, the Sioux suddenly missed their children, and a halt of the caravan was called. But after a few minutes conversation they concluded that, if the Cheyennes were pursuing them, they could not hurt the children. As the rear was crowding them, The Yellow Horse directed that they go on until daylight when they would camp and send a strong party back after the children. So they kept on going.

Daylight came, and still they did not stop but kept traveling until about the middle of the afternoon when they halted from exhaustion. Nothing but rest and food for themselves and animals could be thought of under the circumstances, so they decided to start in search of the forgotten children the next morning.

In the meantime the youngsters had grown weary of their banishment and were waiting patiently during the greater part of the next day to be called back or to secure a visit from some of their relatives. But no one came. Finally some of the older boys went out on their ponies to the top of the ridge where they could get a view of the village and were astounded to see that there was no trace of the hundreds of lodges that they had left there the day before. Hurrying back to their camp they reported the fact to the old women, who constituted the highest authority in this band of children. It was decided to immediately pull up and go back, the old women holding to the hope that the boys were mistaken in the exact location of the lodges and had therefore been taking a view of the wrong place.

Pulling back over the hills with their ponies and travois they were soon undeceived, for, although the sun was fast going down when they came to the last slope down which they had to travel to reach the village they had lately left, they could all plainly see that there was no village there. But keeping on they came to the spot where it had lately stood, when there commenced a mixture of wondering and wailing. It was finally agreed upon to follow the trail, but the question arose which trail, as one led one way and one another. As it was growing dark, they made a choice and began their journey. They traveled all night and rested the next day. In the evening they started again and traveled another night, then rested another day. Starting again in the evening they had traveled about one-third of the night when they saw the fires of the village in a bend of a small creek a short distance ahead of them.

Fearing that the village might belong to the Cheyennes and knowing that the council must have broken up in a row, they halted while three of the older boys crawled up to the lodges to listen to the language that was used by their inmates. They soon returned to their party with the information that they were Cheyennes. Then they turned about and began to retrace their steps.

Their ponies were old, gentle, and tired, and they knew that their safety lay in the fact that the Cheyennes were ignorant of their presence. They traveled back all that night on the same trail they had come over, then rested until noon the next day, when they decided to change their course towards their old camp where the village had been located before moving to meet the Cheyennes, hoping to find their people in that vicinity. But when they arrived at this place, they were disappointed. Growing despondent they gave up their search for their village.

The party had been sent out by The Yellow Horse the second day after their flight, as decided upon, but, when it came to the place where they had located the children, they were nowhere to be found. Giving them up as having been captured by the Cheyennes, they returned to the village disheartened.

The old women acted as the councillors of the new village and encouraged the boys in the art of arrow making and urged them to their best efforts in killing game, the flesh of which was a necessity and the skins of which were made into moccasins, clothing, and lodges. They then passed the first winter. Then the summer following when the older ones began to marry and establish families of their own, tribal organization was effected by the election of the oldest of the young men as their chief with the name of The Yellow Horse.

Seventeen years passed away. This band of youthful warriors had grown strong and powerful. They had met the enemy in battle many times and came off victors but had as yet found no trace of the parent village. But it happened one summer that they had drifted a great deal further north than ever before and were encamped along a small stream in a country that was new to them. Some of their party who were hunting suddenly turning a sharp angle of a hill came almost face-to-face with another party of Indians of about their own number. Each party quickly wheeled and separated a short distance and stopped. Presently one party accosted the other. Each were surprised to find that they spoke the same language. Party number one asked the other who they were, and they replied, "We are Sioux, and we are from a large village a short ride from here, and our chief's name is The Yellow Horse. Who are you?"

"We are Sioux, and our chief's name is The Yellow Horse."

Then party number two asked, "Are you not the lost children?"

Receiving the answer that they were, they consulted a little, then asked them where their village was located. Upon being told they put the whips to their ponies and rode back to their village. When they told the story of having found the lost children, The Yellow Horse, the older, immediately sent out a large party to visit the children, as the old village still called them, and ask them to come home. The answer they sent back to the old village was that they would never return to it as long as The Yellow Horse was alive, that he had cast them away when they were children and now they were men and able to take care of themselves.

This so angered the old chief who immediately declared that he would make them move in and thereupon began to call for warriors. But as the band of the younger

Yellow Horse was looked upon as their children, he could get no volunteers to help him except the members of his own family and their close relations. As these were numerous and great warriors, he concluded to start out with them and carry out his wishes. When he reached the village of the younger Yellow Horse, he was surprised at its size, but he was still only able to remember them as children. Stopping his warriors upon an eminence near the village he sent a messenger in commanding them to take down their lodges and move to his village.

In a short time the messenger returned, bringing a defiant refusal. This so enraged the old man, who for years had been accustomed to use his word as law, that he charged his [the?] village with his party. Young Yellow Horse and his warriors met the charge with a shower of arrows and repulsed them. As they turned after being checked, The Yellow Horse was seen to reel in his saddle, then fall from his horse. Examination proved that he was dead, but no wound could be found upon his body. This was looked upon by the other combatants as some mysterious act of great medicine, and a parley ensued, at which the so-called lost children agreed to move to the village the next day. This they did.

For a long time there was great feasting and rejoicing at the reunion, thus effected after so long a separation. But eventually the tribe began to discuss the election of another chief. Many were in favor of electing the young Yellow Horse as their chief of all the tribe. In fact, the members of his own band would listen to no other proposition. But many were opposed to him, and great dissensions arose among them until it was evident that no chief could be chosen. Then it was suggested that they separate, and each large family group go into a camp by itself and elect its own chief. This they did, and thus it was that the great Western Sioux were divided into so many bands.

Sword's Death in Battle

IT MAY BE FITTING THAT Red Cloud's autobiography draws to a close with another battle against the Crows and with yet another problem in reconciling details of his narrative with other historical sources. No Ears, a nineteenth-century Oglala historian, listed a Crow by the name of Spotted Horse as being killed about 1861 (not in 1863, the date assigned here).[1] In the papers of Amos Bad Heart Bull, another Oglala chronicler, are found two notations, "Many spotted horses. Red Cloud in the party," and, "Spotted Horse was killed." This Crow man was remembered as a courageous leader who, despite a broken leg and being unhorsed, shot down a mounted Lakota (Sword, perhaps?) who was attempting to count coup on him. Elder Lakota informants remembered the incident in the 1930s with a happier ending; before the Crow could drag himself to the fallen warrior, other Lakotas came to the latter's rescue.[2]

With the telling of stories such as has just been related, the long winter nights had been whiled away, and it was in April, 1863, when the incident related in this chapter occurred. The traders had disposed of all their goods and had their wagons loaded ready to pull back to the Post, when one night an Indian by the name of "Sko-We," who had been out for three or four days on a deer hunt, came into camp and immediately reported to the council lodge that he had seen that evening on his way in unmistakable signs of the enemy. Being a very common, easy-going man whose life record consisted principally in staying close to the village and hunting and trapping small game, his information was scouted at and soon dismissed by the more self-sufficient leaders of the village. But the next morning when the village herds were driven in, it was found that they were about five hundred head of horses short. The village was a large one, comprising about five hundred lodges, having been joined at different times during the winter by other bands from the Missouri River, including the Minneconjous, Uncapapas [Hunkpapas], Yanktons, and others. A war party of fully four hundred started in pursuit of the depredators immediately.

Red Cloud was leader of this party, and they followed the trail up a tributary of the Belle Fourche for some distance and were not long in assuring themselves that their horses had been stolen by the Crows. The trail of such a large herd showed plainly, and it could not be driven at a very great rate of speed. The Sioux knew that they were gaining upon them rapidly. In a short time they came to where the creek forked and divided into five different branches. Here they discovered that the Crows had stopped the herd and divided it into as many branches. Each branch of the creek showed a trail going up it made by about one hundred head of horses at full speed. The Sioux quickly divided into four parties. Each party took a different trail, leaving one of the Crow parties unpursued.

Only two of the Sioux parties succeeded in overtaking the Crows. One of these was the party headed by Red Cloud, and the other was under the leadership of Sword. Red Cloud's party gained upon the Crows so closely that they abandoned their horses, and some of them took to the hills and were followed by the Sioux. One Crow who was being closely pursued by Red Cloud and five of his men, jumped from his horse and ran into the brush. He was at once surrounded. Red Cloud, warning his followers not to rush in upon him as some of them were about to do, rode to a point of the timber where the Crow could not see him and from there gave signs to his companions to keep a close watch and wait until he went in and run [ran] the Crow out.

When this was understood, he dismounted, and crawling into the brush and timber he slipped from tree to tree until he saw the Crow standing close beside a large tree. Perceiving that the Crow did not suspect his presence, he crawled nearer and nearer until he was as close to him as he desired to be, then taking good aim, fired. The Crow jumped straight up into the air but failed to fall but began staggering about in a manner that showed Red Cloud that he was only wounded. Fearing that he might recover enough strength to run to another cover, Red Cloud drew his knife and sprang upon him. The wounded and exasperated Crow struck him over the head with his war club, but the stroke overreached, and only the rough raw-hide handle of the club bent itself along the side of Red Cloud's head. The Crow then pulled his knife, but it fell only upon Red Cloud's wrist, while his knife was buried to the hilt in the Crow's vitals. In a few seconds he lay a corpse at the feet of his captor. Red Cloud scalped him and cut off both his ears as further mementoes of the encounter. Red Cloud's companions were not pleased at the result and jealously claimed that he had ordered them to remain outside the timber in order that he might achieve all the notoriety himself.

The party under the leadership of The Sword overtook the Crows also, and a scattering fight ensued. Sword and five or six others who were extra-well mounted were in hot pursuit of a Crow warrior, who, they divined by his actions when first overtaken, was the leader. He had his squaw with him and was mounted upon a very fast horse that the Sioux recognized upon near approach as belonging to Deon—the only horse he had—and it was known to have been missing with the others.

The Crow could have escaped if it had not been for his wife who was not mounted upon so fleet an animal. When they had run a short distance, the Crow would have to check up his horse, wheel back, and commence fighting to protect his wife. While he would be thus engaged in checking the advance of The Sword and his party, he would be making signs in an endeavor to induce his wife to go on and give him an opportunity to overtake her, but she persisted in staying with him. Then they would start together again only to be soon separated by the difference in the speed of their horses, and the Crow would have to charge again to the rear.

After this had been repeated several times, the Crow finally induced his wife to go on. Putting her horse to full speed she was soon lost to view among the hills. The Sword, realizing that the Crow, who was kneeling on one knee reloading and firing, would mount and go again as soon as he thought his wife had gotten far enough ahead to justify it, waited until he had discharged his rifle and began to reload, then dashed upon him. The Crow tried to mount and run, but, just as he swung himself into the saddle, The Sword was upon him and shot him, shattering one of his thighs. The Crow rolled to the ground. The Sword, anxious to count coup upon the fallen enemy before the other Sioux could come up, checked and wheeled his horse as soon as he could and rode back and was just leaning over to strike the Crow when the latter quickly raised an old pistol and shot The Sword through and through in the region of the heart. He fell a corpse by the side of his victim.

The other Sioux were coming up on the run, but they had been so far in the rear of The Sword. Not having any idea of his intentions, the whole incident had occurred so quickly that they were dumbfounded. The Crow still had time, while they were advancing, to rise to a sitting posture and say to them in the sign language, "I am Spotted Horse, chief of the Crows. This is a nice day to die, and I am going but not alone. I take one of you with me." So saying he fell back upon the earth, and in so doing he buried his knife to the hilt in the prostrate form of The Sword. In a minute he was literally chopped to pieces by the enraged Sioux.

While these events were transpiring, the situation at the village was one of anxious waiting. It was about noon of the third day since the departure of the great war party, and some six or eight old men were sitting smoking in Deon's lodge talking, of course, of nothing else but this all absorbing topic. Deon at that time wore a long beard, and he had been sitting on a mat tailor-fashion, gazing into the fire in deep meditation for some time, when all of a sudden, in imitation of some of the Indian peculiarities, he took out his knife and taking hold of the point of his beard cut off about two inches of the end of it and dropping the several hairs into the fire. "I hope the Great Spirit will take pity on me and send back my horse, for it is the only one I have, and I am poor."

The old Indians all laughed at this outburst coming from a white man. But soon it had the significance of a prophecy to them, for in a little while the flap of the lodge door was thrown back, and Red Cloud threw a human ear to Deon, saying, "Here, Foot, is your horse." Deon's Indian name was Foot, and the old Indians, telling him to pick up his horse, rushed out of the lodge to get the news.[3] Many of the warriors had returned, and all the incidents of the trip had been recited. There was great mourning throughout the village over the death of The Sword, who was a nephew of Red Cloud and had numerous relations and was conceded to be one of the bravest young men in the village. His younger brother after his death took the name of Sword and was for years captain of police at Pine Ridge Agency under Agent [Valentine T.] McGillycuddy and is at the present one of the Judges of the Indian Court of the reservation.

About sundown the main body of the great party, consisting of about three hundred, arrived, bringing the corpse with them. Then the people of the village went wild. Frenzied riders rushed among the people and threw down the Crow's head, arms, and feet, which were eagerly gathered up and placed upon the end of poles and hoisted aloft and paraded as trophies of revenge, followed by a wild howling mob of savages, some with their faces painted black and some with their hair cropped off and falling in confusion about their faces, while others would lacerate themselves with the knife as they walked until they made tracks of blood. Every horse and every dog that came in the way of these processions was instantly shot. And between the howling of the dogs as they were either killed or wounded and the yelling and screeching and moaning and groaning of the frenzied mourners, a pandemonium was inaugurated and lasted throughout the night.

The traders were all warned by their friends to keep inside their lodge, with the assurance that, while no one wanted to harm them, some fool acting on sudden impulse might do so. Besides there was so much promiscuous shooting that they would be in danger of being shot accidentally. Acting upon this advice they not only remained inside but took the precaution to line their lodges with a tier of baled buffalo robes, thus making them proof against bullets.

The next day the excitement was considerably subsided, and The Sword had been dressed for burial. He was lying upon a rudely constructed bier, covered with buffalo robes, a short distance from his father's lodge in an open space where all could view him for the last time. He was wrapped in a bright new blanket of scarlet and blue. His hands were folded across his breast. His face was painted a bright vermillion, while his head was decorated with a war bonnet of eagle feathers, the pennant of which was laying gracefully along the entire length of his body and folded over the beaded moccasins on his feet.

While this preparation for burial was in progress, Deon was talking over the matter of getting his horse back with Old American Horse, father of the present chief of the [same] name, and one or two old visitors who were in his lodge. The conversation upon this subject at this time was brought about by the fact that a little girl had just brought his horse up and tied it to his lodge. To a person unaccustomed to Indians and their customs this would seem to indicate that the business pertaining to the recovery of the horse was settled, but he knew too well that this act was only the beginning of the end, that the Indian idea was that The Sword having fought for it, the horse was his, and having died in the fight the horse now belonged to his family, and that as soon as the funeral affairs were over he would be expected to begin paying for his own horse and keep on paying until all the members of the family were satisfied. While he thought a great deal of his horse and wanted it back very much, he did not care to pay for him a dozen times or more. Besides he had nothing left in his possession to pay with, having disposed of every remnant of his goods. And it was this situation that he was talking over with the old men who could devise no way to help him out of the difficulty.

Finally an idea occurred to him, and he submitted it to them. It was to the effect that he take his own gun, a small northwestern trade rifle, and go and present it to The Sword himself. They approved of this plan, saying that it was just what an Indian would do under like circumstances. This plan decided upon, the next thing to be considered was how to get through the crowd that surrounded the body. The old men agreed to go with him, but after a little thought he sent for Red Cloud, who soon put in an appearance. He was in mourning, of course, being naked from his neck to his waist, with his hair falling loosely about his shoulders and a bow and arrow in his hand. He approved of the plan and said he would go first and make the opening through the crowd. Then they started.

Deon was immediately behind Red Cloud, with the old men in the rear. As they passed through the throng, Red Cloud would say, "Make way, my friends. Let me to my dead." And they would quickly part and let him pass. Deon was bare-headed in order that his hat might not attract attention among the sea of heads about him. When they reached the body, they found the immediate members of the family surrounding it.

The Sword's mother and one of his sisters were lying prostrate upon the earth with their faces downward. Two other women holding little children were sitting crying, while his father and brothers were marching around the corpse in the little circular opening with their guns and pistols, shooting sometimes in the ground and sometimes toward the sky and crying and singing, then sometimes lapsing into silence which they would soon break as their mood changed. Their bodies were painted a hideous black over which the blood was streaming from many self-inflicted wounds.

Deon would have given a whole herd of horses at the time to have been out of there, but Red Cloud, walking up to the bier, said, "My nephew, I have brought you a friend." The sound of Red Cloud's voice quieted the other mourners for a moment.

Deon, screwing up his courage, walked to the dead warrior's side and held one hand up to the heavens while with the other he proffered the gun, saying, "My friend, you are a great warrior and a brave man. You died fighting the enemy, and here I give you this gun. Take it along to protect you on your journey and to fight with it in the other world." Setting the gun down against the bier he was greeted with "How, how, how," from the astonished mourners. Turning he soon lost himself among the bystanders and regained his own lodge and was permitted to keep his horse in peace, for he had paid for it heroically and in a manner that appealed to the hearts of those interested. He had paid his respects to their dead in a way that they believed would be beneficial.

After the affairs of the village were again quiet, it was a week before they permitted the traders to depart. During this whole winter the Sioux had been sending and receiving messengers from other tribes and different bands of their own tribe bearing the Pipe of War.[4] The day before the traders left the village they were called to a council and told not to come back to trade again the next winter unless they were sent for, as they were thinking of going to war with the whites. After this they shook hands and parted in peace, taking a good winter's trade of robes with them. The next winter Beauvais & Co. wanted Deon to go out again, but he declined, telling them the reason. As there had been but few depredations committed during the summer by the Oglalas, the company decided to chance two wagonloads of goods anyway, but Deon could not be prevailed upon to go with them, so they sent another man, who was promptly killed and his goods confiscated and his wagons burned.

21

End of the Story

IN MARCH 1932, ADDISON E. SHELDON sent a copy of the Red Cloud autobiography to Luther H. North, a prominent frontiersman. Sheldon considered North a valuable source by virtue of his connection to his more famous brother Frank North, organizer and commander of the Pawnee Scouts, military auxiliaries of the United States Army who had fought the Sioux on numerous occasions. North, who thought his expertise lay exclusively with the Pawnee tribe, deferred to James Cook and his knowledge of Red Cloud and the Sioux. "I was in hopes," wrote North to Cook, "that Red Cloud would tell more about the Powder River wars, 1866–67, than he did."[1] Subsequent historians of the Indian wars, disappointed by the manuscript's omission of this and other subjects important to their studies, have echoed North's lament to Cook. With the beginning of the Oglala's war against the whites, however, came the end of "the Indian part of the life of Red Cloud," as Charles Allen termed it, and the close of the autobiography. A new phase in Red Cloud's life—and more battles—awaited him and his people.

The various depredations committed by the Sioux, Cheyennes, and Arapahos upon frontier settlements and emigrants between the years 1863 and 1868 have not only been recorded but are tales that have been told many times and constitute the greater part of the well understood history of the plains. The part that Red Cloud played during those troubles, sometimes as a great chief and general, was a conspicuous one. But his individual action in the many bloody encounters between his people and the whites must remain forever veiled in obscurity, for the reason that when questioned upon these matters he prefers to maintain a stoical silence. But it is well known that roaming over the country from the South Platte River to the Yellowstone with all the great Sioux nation at his back, except the Brules under Spotted Tail and a few of the extreme northern bands under Sitting Bull, it was his mind that did the planning and his iron will that did the executing of all the important movements.

Determined that the whites and especially the soldiers should leave his country and firmly believing that he was strong enough to force them to do so, he followed this line entirely and would listen to no one suggestion from the government or its agents to the contrary. He strongly opposed the establishment of Camp Connor on the Powder River, afterwards Fort Reno, in 1864 [1865], and fought desperately against the estab-

lishment of Fort Phil Kearney on the Piney and Fort C. F.
Smith on the Big Horn in the spring of 1866. In the
summer of this year, however, he was induced to come
to Fort Laramie where the government commissioners
were treating with the great chief, Spotted Tail, who then
signed a treaty. But all inducements failed to secure Red
Cloud's signature or approval. He told the commissioners plainly that he would make no peace until the whites
vacated the country or until the three military posts just
established should be abandoned and the troops with-
drawn. Returning to the north he made good his word
by planning the attack on Fort Phil Kearney in the fall of
1866, which resulted in the massacre of ninety-two soldiers and one citizen and the death of a large number of
Indians and the disabling of many more by wounds from
which they continued to die for twenty years afterward.

Shortly after this deplorable affair, Forts Phil Kearney,
C. F. Smith, and Reno were abandoned. But the Indians
continued to commit more or less depredations upon
emigrant trains and mining camps until the fall of 1867,
when arrangements were made with Red Cloud to meet
a government commission at Fort Laramie in the spring
of 1868. Hostilities were suspended in the meantime.
John Richard, educated, mixed blood Sioux, was the
courier who went to the hostile camp and effected these
arrangements in the interest of peace. He found Red
Cloud in the vicinity of the Gallatin Valley, Montana, at
the head of an army of three thousand warriors. The
objectionable posts had been abandoned, the most northern wagon trails across the great plains were nearly deserted, the whole country had been terrorized, and it

must have seemed to Red Cloud's unsophisticated mind that there was nothing left for him to conquer. At any rate his people began coming in to Fort Laramie at the time agreed upon, but Red Cloud and the Bad Face band did not come in until the spring of 1869.[2]

The main village stopped at their old camping ground on the North Platte River, north of the post, while Red Cloud, accompanied by a number of his leading warriors, rode into the post to report to the officials. The road that led into the post from the north brought them to the large trader's store, where they halted, dismounted, and tied their ponies. Col. [William G.] Bullock, a citizen and proprietor of the trading establishment, was an old acquaintance of Red Cloud and was always on very sociable terms with him in times of peace. On his arrival he rushed out and proffered him his hand. Red Cloud declined the proffered hand with a significant remark, "Wait, my friend, until I have washed. My hands are bloody to the elbows. I want to wash them before I shake hands with anyone."

And he did so.

The Oglalas remained at the post during the summer. The conditions of the Treaty of 1868 were agreed to by Red Cloud, and, although it has been often broken by both the Indians and the government, it is not believed by anyone who has known and observed Red Cloud through the years that have since passed that he has ever broken that treaty personally by an overt act.

ALL HISTORIANS WOULD AGREE that Red Cloud abided by the provisions of the Fort Laramie Treaty of 1868, and dramatic proof came in spring 1869. At one morning roll call the Fort Laramie garrison awoke to the astounding and unsettling sight of Red Cloud and five hundred of his mounted warriors in possession of the post parade ground! On the surrounding hills watched thousands of his followers.

The post commander belatedly deployed his troops and hurriedly dispatched an interpreter to the Sioux leader to fathom his intentions. According to the Cheyenne, Wyoming, newspaper that carried this story, Red Cloud succinctly replied, "We want to eat."[3] It was food for his hungry people, not war, that had brought him to Fort Laramie. Such concern for their interests repeated itself in the decades to come and showed that Red Cloud, the warrior, had indeed become Red Cloud, the peacemaker.

Appendix A

Editing Procedures

THANKFULLY, CHARLES W. ALLEN published at least a portion of the autobiography before his ill-fated alliance with Addison E. Sheldon. The South Dakota State Historical Society holds five surviving issues of *The Hesperian*, and three contain Allen contributions. Most of chapter 1 appeared in the November 1895 issue of *The Hesperian*. The conclusion of chapter 1 and chapters 2, 3, and 4 appeared in the December 1895 issue; chapter 5 and most of 6 appeared in the following issue in January 1896.

A comparison of *The Hesperian* and the surviving bound typescript at the Nebraska State Historical Society reveals that they are virtually identical. Without the version that preceded Sheldon's involvement, we would never know the extent of his contribution to the document. Mercifully, he added nothing of substance, an important consideration when evaluating the "purity" of the other, unpublished stories. Sheldon's few observations, footnote queries, and tacked-on asides—and typist Mari

Sandoz's typos—are easily detectable and have been filtered out or corrected.

I have remained mindful throughout this process that I follow a long line of "editors" of Red Cloud's autobiography, beginning with Charles Allen and Sam Deon and followed soon thereafter by *The Hesperian*'s Kenneth F. Harris and Allen's correspondent friend, Warren K. Moorehead, who oversaw the conversion of the longhand manuscript to typescript. The list subsequently concluded with Sheldon and Sandoz. Others may step forward from the historical record, although their involvement would prove immaterial and irrelevant if ever Allen's vanished original notes and inked transcription are found. Until they do, readers will have to suffer my effort to remain true to the original as well as to prepare a sensible and reliable text. This involved a number of editorial decisions.

First, the Red Cloud autobiography broke down easily and logically into twenty-one units, for which I have supplied the titles, or chapter headings. Some breaks are apparent in the original text with noticeable white space left between the end of one story and the beginning of another; other stories ran into one another. As with many Native American narratives, most of Red Cloud's stories were rather brief; they did not necessarily follow in strict chronological order, although their original order in the document has been maintained.

Second, Charles Allen never met a conjunction he did not like, no ifs, ands, or buts. He had an aversion to the simple declarative sentence as well as to the paragraph, a somewhat surprising style considering the strictures of newspaper writing that formed his professional background. Furthermore, his use of commas was sporadic if not spastic. Accordingly, I have broken up countless compound sentences and banished dozens of conjunctions without any change to the meaning of the text.

Third and last, the only emendations of note are those involving obvious misspellings and confusing punctuation; with the latter I have sought some semblance of consistency. Also, a few presumed dropped words have been added in brackets, along with the occasional corrected date and the stray editorial comment. I have kept these to a minimum.

Ultimately my contribution to the Red Cloud autobiography rests less with its copy editing and more with documenting its authenticity. This detective story, the uncovering of which has been a thoroughly enjoyable adventure, needed to be fully told. On the other hand, I tried to avoid the trap my predecessor Sheldon fell into. He thought Red Cloud's story needed a full biography wrapped around it, that it could not stand alone, uncluttered. My disagreement takes the form of brief chapter introductions and minimal annotation. Red Cloud has suffered enough from editors.

APPENDIX B

The Charles W. Allen Statement

THIS TRANSCRIPTION OF THE Charles W. Allen statement reads like an affidavit although the four-page typescript was neither signed by Allen or Addison E. Sheldon nor notarized. Unfortunately, no Sheldon diary entry exists for this date to explain the reason for this meeting or to add further details about the Allen-Sheldon collaboration. Nevertheless, the Allen statement confirms Allen's primary role in the autobiography and the methods he employed. The original document is part of the Sheldon Collection, MS 2039, Nebraska State Historical Society, Lincoln.

Mar. 5, 1917.

MR. SHELDON: What Mr. Allen is going to give you is about in this order. The origin of the idea of securing from Red Cloud himself the story of his life, the persons who assisted in putting that idea in action, the time and place at which it was secured from Red Cloud, the persons present when it was secured, the manner in which the Sioux story of Red Cloud was converted into English, the approximate number of days or weeks which Red Cloud spent in relating this story of his life and about how long each day, and any other circumstances which might occur to Mr. Allen including too how any detail and in what way the original manuscript got its authentication.

MR. C. W. ALLEN: The early spring of 1893 I was postmaster at Pine Ridge and familiar and well acquainted with Red Cloud and had been for years, and I conceived the idea of getting the story of his life from him, but knowing his reluctance to exploit himself, having been urged various times by Buffalo Bill to go with the show and spurned each offer, I adopted the following plan of securing the manuscript.

I secured the assistance and services of an old trader, Samuel Deon, who had been with Red Cloud all his life as an Indian trader and knew him well and spoke the language, the Indian Sioux language.

The two used to put in two or three hours a day visiting on the bench by the post office, so I made arrangements with Mr. Deon to begin at the beginning and with questions and queries induced Red Cloud to go over his life from the beginning. They would converse about two hours a day on the average. Immediately at the close of that conversation Mr. Deon would report to me, and I would take down all the facts as notes.

MR. SHELDON: About how long would each conversation with Red Cloud be?

MR. ALLEN: I think I said above on the average of about two hours.

This continued through the whole summer and up to late in the fall, practically six months in duration or until the finish.

These notes were transcribed with ink by my assistant postmaster, W. A. Coffield.

MR. SHELDON: Did you keep the original pencil notes?

MR. ALLEN: I still have them.

MR. SHELDON: Did you keep the original pen and ink notes written by Mr. Coffield from your pencil notes?

MR. ALLEN: I did.

MR. SHELDON: Then, the process by which the information for this manuscript was secured was first by a conversation between Mr. Deon and Red Cloud every day lasting one or two hours. Then immediately at the conclusion of their conversation Mr. Sam Deon dictated to you in English the story which Red Cloud had told him, you writing these notes down in pencil upon paper. Then at what time did you begin dictating these to Mr. Coffield from your pencil notes?

MR. ALLEN: Every day almost immediately after writing my notes.

MR. SHELDON: Then you communicated to Mr. Coffield from your pencil notes the story as you had received it from Mr. Deon; then Mr. Coffield made a pen and ink copy of your notes which was subsequently typewritten. When and where?

MR. ALLEN: These were typewritten by Warren K. Mo[o]rehead at Andover, Mass., Phillips Academy.

MR. SHELDON: He then returned to you the typewritten copy and the original pen and ink copy written by Mr. Coffield, and you have compared them so that you know they are perfectly correct?

MR. ALLEN: I have.

MR. SHELDON: Did Red Cloud know at any time that this was secured from him for the purpose of publication.

MR. ALLEN: He was simply telling the story to a friend.

MR. SHELDON: What did Mr. Deon tell you of the ease or difficulty of getting the story in a chronological form.

MR. ALLEN: Mr. Deon would take up the story as they left it the day before and ask him questions and in this way get him to continue. This Red Cloud manuscript gives the story of Red Cloud up to 1865–1866, the time Red Cloud's tribe went to [on the] war path.

Red Cloud declined to tell the story of the rise of war with the whites because he did not wish to revive those recollections. He claimed that they were past and that they were friends with the whites and that he had no desire to recall his experiences against the whites.

MR. SHELDON: Wasn't a good deal of this life of Red Cloud familiar to Mr. Deon because he had lived many years with Red Cloud?

MR. ALLEN: He wanted them recounted. He wanted to refresh his memory so the two went over them together. Of course he went back farther, prior to the time Deon was with him.

MR. SHELDON: Do you know when Deon first came among the Sioux?

MR. ALLEN: Deon came among the Sioux when he was very young. About twenty. He came from Canada and had lived all his life among the Sioux. Mr. Deon married a Sioux wife and spoke the Sioux language very well. He also spoke French and English. He had a very good command of the English language and spoke it very well.

MR. SHELDON: You have had some newspaper experience and have edited many articles and know about what is covered by a certain number of words. Give your estimate of English on an average of what Mr. Deon would give you each day.

MR. ALLEN: There was 40,000 words in the manuscript, and it took six months.

MR. SHELDON: That would be about 200 words a day or about a sixth of a column.

Notes

INTRODUCTION

1. I draw on Red Cloud's autobiography for the date and place of his birth. See also George Hyde, *Red Cloud's Folk: A History of the Oglala Sioux Indians* (Norman: University of Oklahoma Press, 1937), 317, citing He Dog, Red Cloud's nephew; James R. Walker, *Lakota Society*, ed. Raymond J. DeMallie (Lincoln: University of Nebraska Press, 1982), 88; and "Statements of a Delegation of Ogallala Sioux before the Chairman of the Committee on Indian Affairs, United States Senate, April 29 and 30, 1897, Relative to Affairs at the Pine Ridge Agency, S. Dak.," 55th Cong., 1st sess., *Sen. Exec. Doc.*, vol. 4, no. 61, serial 3561, 9.

2 Richard White, "The Winning of the West: The Expansion of the Western Sioux in the Eighteenth and Nineteenth Centuries," *Journal of American History* 65 (September 1978), 321, 333–34; Kingsley M. Bray, "Teton Sioux Population History, 1655–1881," *Nebraska History* 75 (Summer 1994), 167–68, 177–79. The other five divisions of the Western Sioux are the Blackfeet, Hunkpapa, Miniconjou, Sans Arc, and Two Kettle.

3. James R. Walker, *Lakota Belief and Ritual*, ed. Raymond J. DeMallie and Elaine A. Jahner (Lincoln: University of Nebraska Press, 1980), 137.

4. Anthony McGinnis, *Counting Coup and Cutting Horses: Intertribal Warfare on the Northern Plains, 1738–1889* (Evergreen, Colo.: Cordillera Press, 1990), 51–53, delineates four theaters of war, all in which Red Cloud's Oglalas were active. Colin G.

Calloway, "The Inter-tribal Balance of Power on the Great Plains, 1760–1800," *Journal of American Studies* 16 (April 1982), 25–47, traces how the balance of power shifted to the nomadic tribes.

5. White, "Winning of the West," 336.

6. Eli S. Ricker of Chadron, Nebraska, compiler of eyewitness accounts and personal biographies, interviewed Red Cloud on November 24, 1906, and touched on these subjects. Tablet 25, MS8, Eli S. Ricker Collection (hereafter Ricker Collection), Nebraska State Historical Society Archives, Lincoln (hereafter NSHS). His interpreter was Clarence Three Stars. The Horse Creek Treaty and the Grattan and Blue Water fights are well analyzed in LeRoy R. Hafen and Francis Marion Young, *Fort Laramie and the Pageant of the West, 1834–1890* (Glendale, Calif.: Arthur H. Clark Company, 1938), 177–245; and Robert M. Utley, *Frontiersmen in Blue: The United States Army and the Indian, 1848–1865* (New York: Macmillan, 1967), 112–20.

7. Affidavit of Red Cloud, July 17, 1896, Indian depredation claim of John Richard, No. 3373, Records of the U.S. Court of Claims, Record Group (hereafter RG) 123, National Archives, Washington, D.C. (hereafter NA).

8. Sheldon interviewed Red Fly, a contemporary of Red Cloud, at Pine Ridge on July 30, 1903. The old warrior described his leader as "the chief soldier, the one who managed the war for the Sioux." Red Cloud and Sioux Indians: Material Gathered while on Sioux Reservation and Obtained from Official Reports, 1902–6, MS 2039, Addison E. Sheldon Collection (hereafter Sheldon Collection), NSHS.

9. According to Luther North, Col. Nelson Cole told Frank North that his column had been attacked on September 8, 1865, by Red Cloud himself. George Bird Grinnell, *Two Great Scouts and Their Pawnee Battalion: The Experiences of Frank J. North and Luther H. North, Pioneers in the Great West, 1856–1882, and Their Defence of the Building of the Union Pacific Railroad* (Glendale, Calif.: Arthur H. Clark Company, 1928), 121.

10. Donald K. Adams, ed., "The Journal of Ada A. Vogdes, 1868–71," *Montana The Magazine of Western History* 13 (July 1963), 3. Elsewhere Red Cloud was said to be, in his prime, six feet tall and two hundred pounds.

11. John C. Ewers, "The Image of the White Man as a Glad-hander," *American West* 19 (January/February 1982), 70; James C. Olson, *Red Cloud and the Sioux Problem* (Lincoln: University of Nebraska Press, 1965), chaps. 5, 6.

12. Omaha *Weekly Herald*, June 1, 1870.

13. MS 71, Charles P. Jordan Collection (hereafter Jordan Collection), NSHS. Portions of this Washington speech appeared in the New York *Times*, June 13, 1870.

14. Robert M. Utley, *The Lance and the Shield: The Life and Times of Sitting Bull* (New York: Henry Holt and Company, 1993), 314.

15. Donald Jackson, ed., *Black Hawk, an Autobiography* (Urbana: University of Illinois Press, 1955); S. M. Barrett, ed., *Geronimo's Story of His Life* (New York: Duffield and Company, 1906).

16. Jackson, *Black Hawk*, 24; Barrett, *Geronimo's Story*, xxvii; H. David Brumble III, *An Annotated Bibliography of American Indian and Eskimo Autobiographies* (Lincoln: University of Nebraska Press, 1981), 62–63; H. David Brumble III, *American Indian Autobiography* (Berkeley: University of California Press, 1988), 54.

17. Sheldon asked the questions, and Allen responded in this four-page typescript, dated March 5, 1917. The statement is unsigned and unwitnessed; it has not been previously cited by scholars. Sheldon Collection. These details were no secret to Sheldon. Allen must have told him the entire story earlier, probably during their 1903 meeting. In a 1909 newspaper story after Red Cloud's death, Sheldon gave an embellished account of the Allen-Deon partnership that keeps more or less to the facts covered later in the 1917 statement.

18. Eli Ricker interviewed Sam Deon at Pine Ridge, South Dakota, on November 24, 1906. Tablet 17, Ricker Collection.

19. Allen statement, Sheldon Collection.

20. Grace Raymond Hebard and E. A. Brininstool, *The Bozeman Trail: Historical Accounts of the Blazing of the Overland Routes into the Northwest, and the Fights with Red Cloud's Warriors* (Cleveland: Arthur H. Clark Company, 1922), vol. 2, 186; James H. Cook, *Fifty Years on the Old Frontier as Cowboy, Hunter, Guide, Scout, and Ranchman* (New Haven: Yale University Press, 1923), 213–15.

21. Jordan Collection.

22. James C. Olson, President Emeritus, University of Missouri, to author, August 5, 1993.

23. Brumble's extensive *Annotated Bibliography* and "Supplement" list only two autobiographies written in the third person. H. David Brumble III, "A Supplement to *An Annotated Bibliography of American Indian and Eskimo Bibliographies*,"

Western American Literature 17 (November 1982), 243–60. For observations on the editor-narrator relationship, see Brumble's related work, *American Indian Autobiography*, x, 6, 11; Sally McClusky, "*Black Elk Speaks*, and So Does John Neihardt," *Western American Literature* 6 (Winter 1972), 231–42; and Raymond J. DeMallie, ed., *The Sixth Grandfather: Black Elk's Teachings Given to John G. Neihardt* (Lincoln: University of Nebraska Press, 1984).

24. Tablet 17, Ricker Collection. In tablet 25, Ricker refers to Deon as Peter Abraham Deon, "by long error called 'Samuel' . . . without fault of his own."

25. George Hyde gave Deon's wife's name as Bega and interestingly added that she was a sister of Smoke, Red Cloud's uncle. Hyde, "Appendix: New Notes (1957)," in *Red Cloud's Folk*, 305.

26. Dwelling no. 97, family no. 65, Fort Laramie, Nebraska Territory, Eighth Census of the United States, 1860, NA microfilm pub. no. 653, rl. 665; Charles E. Hanson, Jr., "Geminien P. Beauvais," in LeRoy R. Hafen, ed., *The Mountain Men and the Fur Trade of the Far West* (Glendale, Calif.: Arthur H. Clark, 1969), vol. 7, 39-41; Affidavit of Samuel Deon, October 13, 1892, contained in the Indian depredation claim file of Gememen [sic] P. Beauvais, no. 7099, Records of the U.S. Court of Claims, RG 123, NA.

27. Eugene F. Ware, *The Indian War of 1864* (New York: St. Martin's Press, 1960), 255.

28. The 1868 treaty and others were gathered together in an 1898 report to Congress by the secretary of the interior in "A Report Concerning the Santee Sioux of Nebraska and Flandreau Sioux of South Dakota," 55th Cong., 2d sess., *Sen. Exec. Doc.*, vol. 3, no. 67, serial 3592, 61. The 1891 affidavit is found with claim no. 8, "Records Relating to the Sioux Property Claims, 1891," Records of the Bureau of Indian Affairs, RG 75, NA. See also R. Eli Paul, "Dakota Resources: The Investigation of Special Agent Cooper and Property Damage Claims in the Winter of 1890–1891," *South Dakota History* 24 (Fall/Winter 1994), 212–35; Entry for "Mrs. Dion," Thomas R. Buecker and R. Eli Paul, eds., *The Crazy Horse Surrender Ledger* (Lincoln: Nebraska State Historical Society, 1994), 65.

29. On Charles W. Allen, see "In the West That Was: Memoirs, Sketches, and Legends," MS 2635, Charles W. Allen Collection, NSHS. For excerpts of Allen's autobiography, see

"Red Cloud and the U.S. Flag," *Nebraska History* 21 (October–December 1940), 293–304; and John D. McDermott, "Wounded Knee: Centennial Voices," *South Dakota History* 20 (Winter 1990), 271–83. Allen used portions of the Red Cloud narrative in his autobiography, specifically passages from chapters 18 and 19. For more biographical details, see also "C. W. Allen, Eye Witness to Battle of Wounded Knee, Recalls Early Days," Lincoln (Nebraska) *Sunday Journal and Star*, February 20, 1938; Allen obituary in *Publisher's Auxiliary*, November 28, 1942 (Allen died on November 16).

30. The children of Charles and Emma Allen in 1896 were Nellie, age 21; Joseph, 20; Sophia (elsewhere Sophie), 17; Charles, 15; Samuel, 14; Jessie, 12; Lizzie, 10; Robert, 8; and Julia, 7. "Census of the Sioux and Cheyenne Indians of Pine Ridge Agency, South Dakota/Taken by W. H. Clapp, Captain 16th Infantry, Acting United States Indian Agent, June 30, 1896," transcript in the Sheldon Collection. Three other children preceded their parents in death.

31. On Allen's prominent role in recording the Wounded Knee Massacre see McDermott, "Wounded Knee," 271–83; Don Huls, *The Winter of 1890* (Chadron, Nebr.: Chadron Record, 1974); Richard E. Jensen, R. Eli Paul, and John E. Carter, *Eyewitness at Wounded Knee* (Lincoln: University of Nebraska Press, 1991), 18–19, 44–49, 105, 108, 112, 123–24.

32. Appointment of Postmasters, Records of the U.S. Postal Service, RG 28, NA microfilm pub. no. 841, rl. 117.

33. Chadron *Citizen*, December 21, 1893.

34. C. W. Allen, "Red Cloud, Chief of the Sioux," *The Hesperian* 1 (November 1895, December 1895, January 1896), 144–47, 173–78, 211–16. Mari Sandoz to James C. Olson, July 2, 1964, MS 1047, James C. Olson Collection (hereafter Olson Collection), NSHS; Will G. Robinson, Secretary, South Dakota State Historical Society, Pierre (hereafter SDSHS), to Olson, July 3, 1964, Olson Collection.

35. "Obituary [of Warren K. Moorehead]," *American Antiquity* 5 (July 1939), 65–66.

36. Allen statement, Sheldon Collection.

37. Warren King Moorehead, *The American Indian in the United States: Period 1850–1914, the Present Condition of the American Indian, His Political History and Other Topics* (Andover, Mass.: Andover Press, 1914), 173–80.

38. Sheldon diaries, December 23, 1902, Sheldon Collection.

39. Allen statement, Sheldon Collection; Sheldon diaries, December 27, 1902. Rushville (Nebraska) *Standard*, June 26, 1896, carries a profile of W. A. Coffield. The notes of Sheldon's December 26, 1902, interview of Deon and a story crafted from them and later conversations are found in "Sioux Indian Field Notes," Sheldon Collection.

40. Sheldon diaries, June 16–18, 1903; Red Cloud and Sioux Indians: Material Gathered, Sheldon Collection.

41. *Nebraska State Journal* (Lincoln), December 12, 1909; Addison E. Sheldon to James H. Cook, January 22, 1910, James H. Cook Collection, Agate Fossil Beds National Monument, Harrison, Nebraska; Joseph C. Porter, "Foreword to the Paperback Edition" (1980), in Cook, *Fifty Years*, ix.

42. Sheldon diaries, December 1, 1908.

43. Sheldon to Allen, October 16, 1915, RG 14, Correspondence of Superintendent, NSHS.

44. E. A. Brininstool to James H. Cook, April 16, 1929, Cook Collection. Brininstool and Sheldon's effort resulted in "Chief Crazy Horse, His Career and Death," *Nebraska History* 12 (January–March 1929), 4–78.

45. Sheldon to Cook, October 28, 1931, Cook Collection.

46. Helen Winter Stauffer, *Mari Sandoz, Story Catcher of the Plains* (Lincoln: University of Nebraska Press, 1982), 84–95.

47. Sheldon diaries, February 7, 1938; Allen to Sheldon, November 21, 1938, Correspondence of Superintendent, NSHS.

48. Excerpts appeared in *Publisher's Auxiliary* on November 28 and December 5 at the time of Allen's death in 1942. These were later reprinted in McDermott, "Wounded Knee," 271–83. Sheldon's death ended another unsuccessful attempt to interest a publisher in the reminiscence of Susan Bordeaux Bettelyoun, mixed-blood daughter of the famed Fort Laramie trader James Bordeaux. MS 185, Susan Bordeaux Bettelyoun Collection, NSHS.

49. "James Clifton Olson, Director of the Nebraska State Historical Society, 1946–1956," *Nebraska History* 37 (December 1956), 244–46; Olson, *Red Cloud and the Sioux Problem*, 16n-22n.

50. George E. Hyde to Addison E. Sheldon, September 28, 1931, Sheldon to Hyde, October 10, 1931, W. S. Campbell to Sheldon, November 2, 1928, Sheldon to Campbell, November 5, 1928, Correspondence of Superintendent, NSHS.

51. Utley, *Lance and Shield*, xvi.

52. Mari Sandoz, *Crazy Horse: The Strange Man of the*

Oglalas (New York: Alfred A. Knopf, 1942), 51; Mari Sandoz Collection, University of Nebraska Archives, Lincoln. Mari Sandoz never thought Sheldon would finish the Red Cloud biography, but she dutifully continued sending him material from the National Archives. Stauffer, *Mari Sandoz*, 115, 122; Helen Winter Stauffer, ed., *Letters of Mari Sandoz* (Lincoln: University of Nebraska Press, 1992), 166–69.

53. On Sandoz's unfavorable opinion of Red Cloud, see *Crazy Horse*, 134, 192, 209. Literary scholars may want to compare sometime Sandoz's Crazy Horse to another popular hero of her day. Filmmaker Frank Capra's quiet, reserved, heroic character of John Doe shared a similar destiny to Crazy Horse. Each represented the common man; each was felled by darker forces and treacherous, conspiratorial colleagues. Gary Cooper had Edward Arnold; Crazy Horse had Red Cloud. Capra's movie *Meet John Doe* appeared the year before Sandoz's book *Crazy Horse*.

54. Ibid., viii.

55. Calloway, "Inter-tribal Balance of Power," 30–31.

56. Utley, *Lance and Shield*, 13; McGinnis, *Counting Coup and Cutting Horses*, 210.

57. Red Cloud said this during Washington negotiations with the secretary of the interior on June 10, 1870, a transcription of which James Olson found in the Upper Platte Agency papers, RG 75, NA, and copied. Olson Collection. The speech is paraphrased in the New York *Times*, June 11, 1870.

58. Walker, *Lakota Society*, 72, 73. The literature on Plains Indian warfare is voluminous. See "Bibliographical Essay," in McGinnis, *Counting Coup and Cutting Horses*, 195–215. See also these three classics: John C. Ewers, *The Horse in Blackfoot Indian Culture, with Comparative Material from Other Western Tribes*, Bureau of American Ethnology, Smithsonian Institution Bulletin 159 (Washington, D.C.: Government Printing Office, 1955); Bernard Mishkin, *Rank and Warfare among the Plains Indians*, Monographs of the American Ethnological Society, vol. 3 (New York: J. J. Augustin, 1940); and Frank Raymond Secoy, *Changing Military Patterns on the Great Plains*, Monographs of the American Ethnological Society, vol. 21 (New York: J. J. Augustin, 1953).

59. Royal B. Hassrick, *The Sioux: Life and Customs of a Warrior Society* (Norman: University of Oklahoma Press, 1964), 89–90, 159.

60. Lynne Woods O'Brien, *Plains Indian Autobiographies*, Western Writers Series, no. 10 (Boise: Boise State College, 1973), 7, reasonably draws few distinctions between Native American biography and autobiography.

61. Recent major studies include Brumble, *American Indian Autobiography*; Arnold Krupat, *For Those Who Come After: A Study of Native American Autobiography* (Berkeley: University of California Press, 1985); Arnold Krupat, ed., *Native American Autobiography: An Anthology* (Madison: University of Wisconsin Press, 1994); A. LaVonne Brown Ruoff, *American Indian Literatures: An Introduction, Bibliographic Review, and Selected Bibliography* (New York: The Modern Language Association of America, 1990); Brian Swann and Arnold Krupat, eds., *I Tell You Now: Autobiographical Essays by Native American Writers* (Lincoln: University of Nebraska Press, 1987); and Hertha Dawn Wong, *Sending My Heart Back Across the Years: Tradition and Innovation in Native American Autobiography* (New York: Oxford University Press, 1992).

62. The stock of American Indian autobiography, along with the broader realms of Indian oral history, has risen sharply as such works' invaluable application to studies of Indian-white conflicts have been further demonstrated. Three sterling examples are Richard Allan Fox, Jr., *Archaeology, History, and Custer's Last Battle* (Norman: University of Oklahoma Press, 1993); Jerome A. Green, ed., *Lakota and Cheyenne: Indian Views of the Great Sioux War, 1876–1877* (Norman: University of Oklahoma Press, 1994); and John D. McDermott, *Forlorn Hope: The Battle of White Bird Canyon and the Beginning of the Nez Perce War* (Boise: Idaho State Historical Society, 1978).

63. David Brumble and Arnold Krupat, "Autobiography," in *Dictionary of Native American Literature,* ed. Andrew Wiget (New York: Garland Publishing, 1994), 176; Krupat, *Native American Autobiography,* 15; James H. Howard, ed., *The Warrior Who Killed Custer: The Personal Narrative of Chief Joseph White Bull* (Lincoln: University of Nebraska Press, 1968); Wooden Leg, *A Warrior Who Fought Custer,* ed. Thomas B. Marquis (Minneapolis: The Midwest Company, 1931); Lucullus Virgil McWhorter, *Yellow Wolf: His Own Story* (Caldwell, Idaho: Caxton Printers, 1940).

64. Frank B. Linderman, *Plenty-coups, Chief of the Crows* (Lincoln: University of Nebraska Press, 1962), 311. See also Peter Nabokov, *Two Leggings: The Making of a Crow Warrior* (New York: Thomas Y. Crowell Company, 1967), 197.

65. Brumble, *American Indian Autobiography*, 4; Brumble and Krupat, "Autobiography," 179–80.
66. Jackson, *Black Hawk*, 28.

CHAPTER 1. THE COMING CHIEF

1. In his early article, "On the Comparative Phonology of Four Siouan Languages," *Annual Report of the Smithsonian Institution for the Year 1883* (Washington, D.C.: Government Printing Office, 1885), 919, James Owen Dorsey specifically stated that "the Bureau of Ethnology of the Smithsonian Institution has adopted the new term 'Siouan,' as the name of this family."
2. Brumble, *American Indian Autobiography*, 49; Ulysses S. Grant, *Personal Memoirs of U.S. Grant*, 2 vols. (New York: Charles L. Webster and Company, 1885–86).
3. The period during which Red Cloud's Oglalas concentrated their attentions on the Pawnee tribe is examined on a yearly basis in Benjamin R. Kracht, "The Effects of Disease and Warfare on Pawnee Social Organization, 1830–1859: An Ethnohistorical Approach" (M.A. thesis, University of Nebraska, Lincoln, 1982).
4. To see distances given in this and the other stories in "miles," an English, not a Lakota, standard of measurement, is rather puzzling. Who was providing them? Plains Indian narrators commonly referred to distances between points as so many days' travel. Here Red Cloud's home was more fittingly given as a seven days' march from the Pawnee village. Captain William Philo Clark, a veteran of the Great Sioux War of 1876–1877, commented on this cultural difference at length. W. P. Clark, *The Indian Sign Language* (Philadelphia: L. R. Hamersly and Company, 1885), 151.
5. For a description of the return of another successful war party to its village, see *The Sioux*, 82–84.

CHAPTER 2. AMBUSH

1. McGinniss's fourth chapter, "Their Name is a Terror: Warfare in Blackfoot and Crow Country, 1830–1850," in *Counting Coup and Cutting Horses*, covers the competition between the two tribes for these two decades. For the events of the following decade, see Kingley M. Bray, "Lone Horn's Peace: A

New View of Sioux-Crow Relations, 1851–1858," *Nebraska History* 66 (Spring 1985), 28–47.

2. Lewis Bissell Dougherty, a young Missouri trader, believed he had met Red Cloud at Fort Laramie in the early 1850s. Ethel Massie Withers, ed., "Experiences of Lewis Bissell Dougherty on the Oregon Trail, Part III," *Missouri Historical Review* 25 (October 1930), 110–12.

3. For descriptions of the typical Crow raiding party, see Robert H. Lowie, *The Crow Indians* (New York: Farrar and Rinehart, 1935), 218–27.

CHAPTER 3. WAR WITH THE OMAHAS

1. Details on Omaha warfare and defensive measures taken while on their seasonal buffalo hunts are found in Alice C. Fletcher and Francis La Flesche's classic *Omaha Tribe*, Twenty-seventh Annual Report of the Bureau of American Ethnology, 1905–1906 (Washington, D.C.: Government Printing Office, 1911), 100, 275, 402, 423–31.

2. The sign language of the Plains Indians strongly impressed the previously cited Captain Clark, Second U.S. Cavalry, who wrote *Indian Sign Language*. More than a mere dictionary, his study also included considerable ethnological and historical details about its users.

CHAPTER 4. RAID ON THE CROWS

1. White, "Winning of the West," 336–37.

2. Joseph Medicine Crow, *From the Heart of the Crow Country: The Crow Indians' Own Stories* (New York: Orion Books, 1992), 62.

3. Red Cloud would not have been surprised to see a Crow herder so far from camp. The Crows were known for taking good care of their horses. Edwin Thompson Denig, *Five Indian Tribes of the Upper Missouri: Sioux, Arikaras, Assiniboines, Crees, Crows*, ed. John C. Ewers (Norman: University of Oklahoma Press, 1961), 145.

4. Trader Dougherty gave yet another example of a remarkably high horse-to-herder ratio. He witnessed six Pawnee raiders successfully herd 120 head of stolen horses to their home

village. Ethel Massie Withers, ed., "Experiences of Lewis Bissell Dougherty on the Oregon Trail, Part II," *Missouri Historical Review* 24 (July 1930), 563-65.

CHAPTER 5. SHOSHONES

1. Not surprisingly, Plains Indians preferred rifles to smoothbore guns, and the market price reflected this. Louis A. Garavaglia and Charles G. Worman, *Firearms of the American West, 1803–1865* (Albuquerque: University of New Mexico Press, 1984), 355.

2. Charles E. Hanson, *The Hawken Rifle: Its Place in History* (Chadron, Nebr.: The Fur Press, 1979). Interestingly, Frank Grouard's biography, another as-told-to work concerning a contemporary of Red Cloud, mentioned the Sioux leader Sitting Bull as also owning a "Hawkins." Joe DeBarthe, *Life and Adventures of Frank Grouard*, ed. Edgar I. Stewart (Norman: University of Oklahoma Press, 1958), 39.

3. Colin C. Calloway, "Snake Frontiers: The Eastern Shoshones in the Eighteenth Century," *Annals of Wyoming* 63 (Summer 1991), 91-92; John D. Unruh, Jr., *The Plains Across: The Overland Emigrants and the Trans-Mississippi West, 1840–60* (Urbana: University of Illinois Press, 1979), 160.

4. The summer of 1849 emigration and attendant perils are mentioned in Hyde, *Red Cloud's Folk*, 63-64. Hyde has Red Cloud's village located on the White River in present-day southwest South Dakota.

5. Shinny ball, played with stick and ball, somewhat resembles field hockey.

6. Big Spider appears in other historical documents as "Spider." Lt. Joseph H. Dorst's letter from Camp Robinson, Nebraska, to 1st Lt. Jesse M. Lee, Camp Sheridan, Nebraska, dated March 23, 1877, mentioned the presence of "Spider, Red Cloud's brother." General Correspondence, Rosebud Agency, RG 75, National Archives–Central Plains Region, Kansas City. See also Buecker and Paul, eds., *Crazy Horse Surrender Ledger*, 152.

CHAPTER 6. SHOOTING BULL BEAR

1. Francis Parkman, Jr., *The Oregan Trail*, ed. E. N. Feltskog (Lincoln: University of Nebraska Press, 1994), 157–59;

Rufus B. Sage, *Rocky Mountain Life, or, Startling Scenes and Perilous Adventures in the Far West, during an Expedition of Three Years* (1846, 1857; reprinted from the 1857 edition, Lincoln: University of Nebraska Press, 1982), 121; American Horse's winter count for 1841–42, in Garrick Mallery, *Picture-writing of the American Indians*, Tenth Annual Report of the Bureau of Ethnology to the Secretary of the Smithsonian Institution, 1888–89 (Washington, D.C.: Government Printing Office, 1893), 568; Iron Crow's winter count for 1841, Walker, *Lakota Society*, 140.

2. For another account of the origin of the Kiyuksa/Koya/Cut-off Oglala band, see the Ricker interview of William Garnett at Cane Creek, South Dakota, January 10, 1907, Tablet 1, Ricker Collection.

3. Hyde dismissed Charles Eastman's assertion that the Ute tribe and Red Cloud's Oglalas were at war in the 1840s, incorrectly it now seems because Red Cloud's account clearly backs up Eastman. Hyde, *Red Cloud's Folk*, 88.

4. Little Wound, Bull Bear's son (not his nephew as stated later in this story), gave a few biographical details on Bull Bear that appear in Walker, *Lakota Belief and Ritual*, 195. Artist Alfred Jacob Miller painted Bull Bear in 1837, and the original watercolor hangs at the Walters Art Gallery in Baltimore. Marvin C. Ross, *The West of Alfred Jacob Miller* (Norman: University of Oklahoma Press, 1968), plate 45.

5. The later, surprisingly cordial relationship between Red Cloud and Little Wound, the chief of the Kiyuksa band after 1870, was described in Garnett's interview. In a profile of Red Cloud for the Omaha *World-Herald*, March 8, 1896, a correspondent, presumably a Pine Ridge Reservation resident, wrote that "although bitter hatred existed between the two for many years it had long since passed away."

CHAPTER 7. RAID ON THE PAWNEES

1. Rancher and author James Cook's close friendship with Red Cloud is detailed in Dorothy Cook Meade, *Heart Bags and Hand Shakes: The Story of the Cook Collection* (Lake Ann, Mich.: National Woodlands Publishing Company, 1994).

2 Pawnee missionaries left excellent accounts of the relentless attacks conducted by Sioux raiders. "Letters Concerning the Presbyterian Mission in the Pawnee Country, near Bellevue,

Neb., 1831–1849," *Collections of the Kansas State Historical Society, 1915–1918* (1918), vol. 14, 570–784.

3. According to Cook, the arrow "was driven through the center of his body from front to back, so that the head of the shaft projected beyond the barbs. His medicine men pulled the arrow through, and for three days and nights he lay like a dead man, with hardly enough heart action to be felt." Cook, *Fifty Years*, 202.

CHAPTER 8. MARRIAGE

1. Sioux practices in courting, marriage, and polygamy are described in Hassrick, *The Sioux*, 111–21; and Raymond J. DeMallie, "Male and Female in Traditional Lakota Culture," in *The Hidden Half: Studies of Plains Indian Women*, ed. Patricia Albers and Beatrice Medicine (Lanham, Md.: University Press of America, 1983), 250–55.

2. Brumble, *American Indian Autobiography*, 59.

3. For more on Fort Laramie as a magnet for the Sioux and other Plains tribes, see Bray, "Teton Sioux Population History," 181; Bray, "Lone Horn's Peace," 28–29, 36–37; and James A. Hanson, "A Forgotten Fur Trade Trail," *Nebraska History* 68 (Spring 1987), 4.

4. This means of suicide was not unprecedented. Susan Bordeaux Bettelyoun, born in 1857 and living at Fort Laramie, recalled an acquaintance, a young mixed-blood Lakota girl, who in 1865 hanged herself in response to a chastisement by her mother. "Autobiography of Susan Bordeaux Bettelyoun, a Story of the Oglala and Brule Sioux," 259–60, Bettelyoun Collection.

5. Charles Jordan provided a rare quotation that can be attributed to Pretty Owl, spoken during a 1902 visit of the Red Clouds to Jordan's Rosebud Agency, South Dakota, home.

"[L]ooking at Red Cloud, she said jokingly, 'When he was a young man, I was very jealous of him and used to watch him very closely for fear some other woman would win him from me.' Red Cloud seemed to enjoy the joke, and added, 'Yes, she surely kept on my trail.' " Jordan Collection.

CHAPTER 9. FAILURE

1. Charles E. Hanson, Jr., "The Mexican Traders," *The Museum of the Fur Trade Quarterly* 6 (Fall 1970), 2–6; James A.

Hanson, "Spain on the Plains," *Nebraska History* 74 (Spring 1993), 6–7, 19.

2. Present in Lakota society were several categories of ritual specialists, this particular "medicine man" representing but one. They are described in William K. Powers, *Oglala Religion* (Lincoln: University of Nebraska Press, 1975), chap. 6, and Powers, *Sacred Language: The Nature of Supernatural Discourse in Lakota* (Norman: University of Oklahoma Press, 1986), chap. 7. For a description by a *wicasa wakan* (holy man or shaman) who went to war, see also Walker, *Lakota Belief and Ritual*, 74–80.

3. Father Pierre-Jean De Smet, the noted missionary and western traveler, commented on the degree of respect that the Plains tribes held for the grizzly bear. De Smet, *Western Missions and Missionaries: A Series of Letters* (New York: James B. Kirker, 1863), 139. See also Miller's written descriptions in Ross, *West of Alfred Jacob Miller*, plates 32, 107, 125.

4. The Omaha dance is also known as the grass dance. The Sioux learned it from the Omaha tribe. Frances Densmore, *Teton Sioux Music*, Bureau of American Ethnology, Smithsonian Institution Bulletin 61 (Washington, D.C.: Government Printing Office, 1918), 468–77.

5. Sacred stones and their associated ceremonies and songs are extensively reported in ibid., 204–44, 348.

CHAPTER 10. SCALPED ALIVE

1. John C. Ewers, *The Blackfeet: Raiders on the Northwestern Plains* (Norman: University of Oklahoma Press, 1958), chap. 7, examines the raids by the Blackfeet on the Crows and other adversaries during the mid-nineteenth century.

2. Red Cloud's trip to Fort Benton cannot be confirmed.

3. Ewers, *The Blackfeet*, 139, mentions other Blackfeet Indians who survived scalping and returned to their people. Some cultures considered the survivor "ruined" and forced him or her to live a solitary life. Douglas R. Parks, "An Historical Character Mythologized: The Scalped Man in Arikara and Pawnee Folklore," in *Plains Indian Studies: A Collection of Essays in Honor of John C. Ewers and Waldo R. Wedel*, ed. Douglas H. Ubelaker and Herman J. Viola (Washington, D.C.: Smithsonian Institution Press, 1982), 48–49; Melvin R. Gilmore, "The Plight of Living Scalped Indians," *Papers of the Michigan Academy of Science, Arts, and Letters* 19 (1933), 39–45.

CHAPTER 11. THE PIPE DANCE

1. For descriptions of the Hunka, see Walker, *Lakota Belief and Ritual*, 193–241, passim; Helen H. Blish, *A Pictographic History of the Oglala Sioux* (Lincoln: University of Nebraska Press, 1967), 425-32; and Densmore, *Teton Sioux Music*, 68–77. Francis Parkman may have said it best and most succinctly for Red Cloud and other aspiring Sioux, "One wishing to be a chief feasts the nation and gives away all he has in presents." Mason Wade, ed., *The Journals of Francis Parkman* (New York: Harper and Brothers Publishers, 1947), vol. 2, 444, 449.

2. Jordan Collection; C. P. Jordan to Doane Robinson, June 26, 1902, H74.9, Doane Robinson Papers (hereafter Robinson Papers), SDSHS; "Chief Red Cloud Makes Last Visit to His Friend, Col. Charles P. Jordan," Omaha *World-Herald*, August 31, 1902; letter from Mrs. John R. Brennan to Robinson, May 7, 1904, concerning the names of Red Cloud's children, Robinson Papers; heirship report, H78-16, Red Cloud Estate Papers, SDSHS. Autobiographical details on Jack Red Cloud appeared in Joseph K. Dixon, *The Vanishing Race: The Last Great Indian Council* (Garden City: Doubleday, Page and Company, 1913), 118-21. His tombstone is illustrated in Veryl Walstrom, *My Search for the Burial Sites of Sioux Nation Chiefs* (Lincoln: Dageforde Publishing, 1995), 144.

3. A voluminous record exists for the 1854–1856 events in Sioux country. One should begin with Utley, *Frontiersmen in Blue*, 115–20.

4. Grand gatherings of the Sioux usually were held in the summer. One such council occurred near Bear Butte, north of the Black Hills, in the summer of 1857. Hyde, *Red Cloud's Folk*, 82; Gouverneur K. Warren, *Preliminary Report of Explorations in Nebraska and Dakota, in the Years 1855–'56–'57* (Washington, D.C.: Government Printing Office, 1875), 52.

5. Allen's Oglala "aristocracy" may refer to the high-ranking chief's society, from which the leaders of the tribe were chosen. Membership was partially hereditary, partially based on merit. Walker, *Lakota Society*, 39; Clark Wissler, *Societies and Ceremonial Associations in the Oglala Division of the Teton-Dakota*, Anthropological Papers of the American Museum of Natural History, vol. 11, pt. 1 (1912), 7.

CHAPTER 12. TO WHIP A DOG

1. "Our people have no recollection of ever having been at war with the Sioux," wrote Cheyenne mixed-blood George Bent late in his life. George E. Hyde, *Life of George Bent Written from His Letters*, ed. Savoie Lottinville (Norman: University of Oklahoma Press, 1968), 22.

2. Walker, *Lakota Society*, 28-34; Wissler, "Societies and Ceremonial Associations in the Oglala Division," 8–10, 13–36.

CHAPTER 13. DECOYING THE CROWS

1. Catherine Price, *The Oglala People, 1841–1879: A Political History* (Lincoln: University of Nebraska Press, 1996), 67–69.

2. A winter count kept by a member of Red Cloud's village and interpreted by a later tribal historian told of Red Cloud leading a war party against the Crow in 1857, close to the year attributed to this story. William K. Powers, "A Winter Count of the Oglala," *American Indian Tradition* 9 (no. 1, 1963), 31.

3. Young Man Afraid of His Horse was one of the last four Oglala shirt wearers, arguably the most respected honor in the society. Any rivalry between Red Cloud and Young Man Afraid ended in 1893 with the latter's death. Chadron *Citizen*, July 20, 1893; Omaha *World-Herald*, August 2, 1893.

CHAPTER 14. ESCAPE BY BOAT

1. For information on the Arikara tribe in the 1850s, see Roy W. Meyer, *The Village Indians of the Upper Missouri: The Mandans, Hidatsas, and Arikaras* (Lincoln: University of Nebraska Press, 1977), 103–9.

2. George Metcalf, "The Bull Boats of the Plains Indians and the Fur Trade," *The Museum of the Fur Trade Quarterly* 8 (Summer 1972), 1–10.

3. John P. Williamson, *An English-Dakota Dictionary* (St. Paul: Minnesota Historical Press, 1992).

4. These were "Gros Ventres of the Prairie" or the Atsina tribe, kinsmen to the Arapahos. They are not to be confused with the Hidatsa tribe, kinsmen to the Crows, and also designated at times as "Gros Ventres of the Missouri." Frederick Webb Hodge, *Handbook of American Indians North of Mexico, Part 1*, Bureau of American

Ethnology, Smithsonian Institution Bulletin 30 (Washington, D.C.: Government Printing Office, 1907), 113, 508.

5. These may be Lower Brulés, who in the late 1850s typically lived near the mouth of the White River in South Dakota. Ernest L. Schusky, *The Forgotten Sioux: An Ethnohistory of the Lower Brule Reservation* (Chicago: Nelson-Hall, 1975).

CHAPTER 15. REVENGE

1. Eleanor H. Hinman, "Oglala Sources on the Life of Crazy Horse," *Nebraska History* 57 (Spring 1976), 10.

2. Brought to my attention by historian James A. Hanson, the sketch of Scalp Mountain can be found in the papers of James Hall, a friend of Hayden's and a fellow geologist, in the New York State Library, Albany. See also Mike Foster, *Strange Genius: The Life of Ferdinand Vandeveer Hayden* (Niwot, Colo.: Roberts Rinehart Publishers, 1994).

CHAPTER 16. THE SNAKE FORT

1. Charles E. Hanson, Jr., "The Battle of Crow Butte," *The Museum of the Fur Trade Quarterly* 5 (Fall 1969), 2-4.

2. Interview of Francis Salway by Addison E. Sheldon, July 31, 1903, Sheldon Collection.

CHAPTER 17. TRADERS

1. Deon interview in "Sioux Indian Field Notes," Sheldon Collection.

2. For a description of a Murphy freighting wagon, see Emily Ann O'Neil Bott, "Joseph Murphy's Contribution to the Development of the West," *Missouri Historical Review* 47 (October 1952), 18–28.

3. In the late 1850s a Cheyenne man remarked to a German missionary, "The wolves are gone. The whites have killed them with their poison." Gerhard M. Schmutterer, *Tomahawk and Cross: Lutheran Missionaires among the Northern Plains Tribes, 1858–1866* (Sioux Falls, S.D.: The Center for Western Studies, 1989), 93.

4. During his life the great Red Cloud did not escape being soldiered. Once he refused the order of an *akicita* to break camp and was lashed until he submitted. Walker, *Lakota Society*, 87.

CHAPTER 18. THE WHISKEY PEDDLER

1. Recent studies on alcohol's corrosive effect in the fur trade are Tanis C. Thorne, "'Liquor Has Been Their Undoing': Liquor Trafficking and Alcohol Abuse in the Lower Missouri Fur Trade," *Gateway Heritage* 13 (Fall 1992), 4–23; and William E. Unrau, *White Man's Wicked Water: The Alcohol Trade and Prohibition in Indian Country, 1802–1892* (Lawrence: University Press of Kansas, 1996).

2. Walker, *Lakota Belief and Ritual*, 138; Jordan Collection.

3. Note Allen's rare insertion here of a first-person comment, induced, no doubt, by his desire to defend Red Cloud's reputation.

CHAPTER 19. THE LOST CHILDREN

1. Brumble, *American Indian Autobiography*, 175.

2. Walker, *Lakota Society*, 11.

3. Agnes Wright Spring, *Caspar Collins: The Life and Exploits of an Indian Fighter of the Sixties* (New York: Columbia University Press, 1927), 174–77.

4. Nick Janis, who married into the Red Cloud family, came from a family of fur traders. Janet Lecompte, "Antoine Janis," in *The Mountain Men and the Fur Trade of the Far West*, ed. Leroy R. Hafen (Glendale, Calif.: Arthur H. Clark Company, 1971), vol. 8, 196–201; John S. Collins, *My Experiences in the West*, ed. Colton Storm (Chicago: The Lakeside Press, 1970), 145–47.

5. The Sioux designated the Cheyenne tribe as the "Cut Fingers," which elsewhere appears in the historical record as "cut arms" and "gashed and cut people." Apparently all arose from the self-mutilation practiced by mourning tribal members. George Bird Grinnell, *The Cheyenne Indians: Their History and Ways of Life* (New York: Cooper Square Publishers, 1962), vol. 1, 3–4; Clark, *Indian Sign Language*, 98–99.

6. Cheyenne origins east of the Missouri River appear in the archaeological record most demonstrably in W. Raymond Wood, *Biesterfeldt: A Post-Contact Coalescent Site on the Northeastern Plains*, Smithsonian Contributions to Anthropology 15 (Washington, D.C.: Smithsonian Institution Press, 1971). This study also surveys the tribe's ethnohistory regarding its origins.

7. One difference in the two accounts is that Collins had a Sioux man running off with a Cheyenne woman. Spring, *Caspar Collins*, 175.

CHAPTER 20. SWORD'S DEATH IN BATTLE

1. Walker, *Lakota Society*, 144.

2. Blish, *Pictographic History of the Oglala Sioux*, 502–3. As with Red Cloud, Amos Bad Heart Bull recorded with equal candor Sioux victory and defeat.

3. Sam Deon referred to himself as "Stinking Feet," the name given to him by his Sioux friends. "Sioux Indian Field Notes," Sheldon Collection.

4. George Bent remembered seeing the war pipe sent from the Western Sioux to his Cheyenne camp during the winter of 1863–1864. Hyde, *Life of George Bent*, 119–21.

CHAPTER 21. END OF THE STORY

1. Sheldon to North, March 9, 1932, MS 449, Luther H. North Collection, NSHS; North to Cook, March 19, 1932, Cook Collection.

2. In her diary Ada Vogdes set the date of Red Cloud's arrival at Fort Laramie as November 5, 1868. Adams, "Journal of Ada A. Vogdes," 3–4. Red Cloud did not sign the treaty until the next year.

3. *Wyoming Weekly Leader* (Cheyenne), April 3, 1868.

Index